Developing Employee Talent to Perform

Developing Employee Talent to Perform

People Power

Kim Warren

business**expert**
Press

Developing Employee Talent to Perform

First published by Vola Press Ltd., London 2005

Published in 2009 by
Business Expert Press, LLC
222 East 46th Street, New York, NY 10017
www.businessexpertpress.com

ISBN-13: 978-1-60649-039-6 (paperback)
ISBN-10: 1-60649-039-7 (paperback)

ISBN-13: 978-1-60649-040-2 (e-book)
ISBN-10: 1-60649-040-0 (e-book)

DOI 10.4128/9781606490402

A publication in the Business Expert Press Human Resource Management and Organizational Behavior collection

Collection ISSN (print) 1946-5637
Collection ISSN (electronic) 1946-5645

Cover design by Artistic Group—Monroe, NY
Interior design by Scribe, Inc.

First edition: April 2009

10 9 8 7 6 5 4 3 2 1

Printed in the United States of America.

Abstract

People are an expensive, critical resource in any organization and can be a powerful source of sustained advantage. They profoundly affect other resources, including customers, brand reputation, intellectual property, and cash. They drive the growth or decline of these resources and possess attributes of their own—such as skills and knowledge—that must be carefully developed and nurtured.

Despite this, leaders tend to focus on the softer aspects of people management, those that are the least easy to identify and influence, such as motivating, mentoring, and team-working—while ignoring the simpler fundamentals of how many they need, where, over time, to do what. *Developing Employee Talent to Perform* redresses the balance, providing a practical, fact-based approach to managing this most sensitive of resources.

This book does the following:

- shows leaders how to understand and manage the changes in their staff-base over time, in the light of often complex interactions between hiring, promotion, development, and attrition
- explains where people connect to the tangible resources of the business, to help ensure they are deployed more effectively, getting the right number of the best people in the right places and adapting these deployments as the business changes through time
- describes the mechanisms by which people and teams develop skills and shared capabilities, so that they can bring about substantially improved performance for the organization as a whole
- provides a common language, in diagrams, words, and numbers, for leaders, HR professionals, and others in the management team to understand and communicate about how their staff resources are developing through time, ensuring that expensive and effort-intensive initiatives to develop the organization can be undertaken with confidence and support

The book gives clear explanations and illustrations of the key concepts, with action checklists, key questions, and case examples.

A strong understanding of how individuals interact with other resources to make the whole organization perform will help managers see how to act to maximize the effectiveness with which their organization operates. Improving performance through better decision making about your organization's people is not just a matter for top management: Given the right tools, anyone with influence over how his or her enterprise works can make a difference. This book provides an original, rigorous, yet practical approach to developing organizational effectiveness that is long overdue.

Keywords

Strategic management, human resources, talent, staffing, business strategy, strategy implementation, strategy dynamics, employer brand

Contents

Introduction

Much has been written about the importance of people in the success of businesses and organizations. Yet the links between people issues and performance outcomes are rarely made clear. Strategy and policy are usually treated in a generalized way, with checklists and descriptive diagrams instead of factual information about what is going on and why. Similarily, the understanding of how people and organizations develop and adapt through time is confined to a simple qualitative focus. Small wonder, then, that this crucial area remains shrouded in mystery.

This lack of clarity makes it hard to understand how managers' choices will drive their organization's progress into the future. It also poses problems for human resource professionals when they try to explain how their efforts to grow and sustain their people will actually work. The simple conviction that such efforts and investments must be "a good thing" is increasingly inadequate for winning the support and commitment of colleagues in other parts of the business; to give you that support, they need evidence.

This book bridges the understanding gap from both directions:

- It provides the basic tools to construct a fact-based picture of how the scale of an organization's pool of people changes through time.
- It explains how to capture the solid resources at the heart of any enterprise and reveals the basic mechanisms by which they depend on each other to develop (Warren, 2008).

This contribution to understanding organizational performance and people makes use of an underlying framework that is both rigorous and practical, known as strategy dynamics. Building on this solid foundation clarifies the links between organizational groups and the business levers they control. Armed with this understanding, you will be able to understand how people-oriented initiatives in your organization will develop through time, track and adjust those initiatives to keep them on course, and trace their impact on your goals.

However, we do not neglect the soft factors that are such powerful drivers of performance. This book enables you to understand, measure, and manage intangible factors shared by your people, such as morale and capabilities, as well as those that occur in other parts of the business, such as reputation among customers and investors. You will also see how to depict these soft factors in a way that gives them substance and connects them to the underlying engine of enterprise performance.

With practice, you and your colleagues will be able to use the tools in this book to inform your discussions about the effort and investment that must go into developing and supporting your people. The result will be better decisions about this important and costly issue and much greater confidence in your organization's ability to deliver the outcomes you desire.

CHAPTER 1

People, Resources, and Performance

Overview

Every organization faces the challenge of building performance over time, whether measured by financial results or other outcomes. Your resources are fundamental to accomplishing this continuing goal, so good strategic management requires a deep understanding of what exactly resources are, how they develop and interact over time, and the skilled design and control of these processes. This chapter explains how your business's strategy toward its people works through the other parts of the strategy to deliver performance results. This chapter explains the following:

- **how resources drive performance** and what "performance" means for business and other organizations; it is not an abstract, qualitative notion but a factual, quantitative concept
- **how people are intimately involved in delivering performance** by winning, developing, maintaining, and using the other resources

Resources Drive Performance

Before we start exploring how people-related issues develop through time, it is worth reminding ourselves exactly why we are doing this. In business situations, investors are not *primarily* concerned with your people; they are largely investing for a financial return. In nonprofit situations, such as public services and voluntary organizations, those who provide funding and support are primarily concerned with what they expect your people to *achieve* rather than with the people themselves. Investors and supporters may, of course, take into account the way your organization treats people in pursuit of its performance aims, but it is these aims that are the main focus of attention. Even your own staff, if they have a personal stake in your organization's performance, will not thank you for looking after them nicely today if it means the enterprise fails tomorrow.

It is common to hear managers insist, "We could easily deliver better performance if only we had the resources." This is true in a far more literal sense than is often realized: Resources genuinely drive an organization's performance. Competition and other pressures may, of course, constrain what you can achieve, but for any set of external conditions, the supply of available resources *directly* determines performance. This is easiest to understand in a business context.

The "performance" we are concerned with is most often profits, and we would generally prefer these profits to grow, strongly and sustainably, into the future. Clearly, profits depend on sales revenue and costs. Sales depend on numbers of customers, and costs reflect the scale of capacity, systems, staff, product range, and other factors. These items (including customers) are all, strictly speaking, resources: valuable assets that have been built up over time and must be maintained.

Of course, we would prefer to keep the sales revenues without the other costly resources, but that is not realistic. Trying to get away with fewer staff or products and less capacity than we really need will ultimately lead us to lose customers and sales. If we want more customers and revenue, then we usually need more of those costly resources. So managers are right: They genuinely *could* deliver better performance if they had more resources.

We will explain later how these factors together make up the business machine—or "architecture"—that drives performance, but the basic idea that profits depend on resources is sufficient for now (Collis & Montgomery, 1994). Similar principles apply to public services, voluntary bodies, and other nonprofit organizations. Their ability to meet the demands made on them depends on their having the necessary capacity, people, and service offerings.

The Part That People Play

So where do people fit in all this? Without them, things would fall apart. People are pivotal to winning, keeping, and using resources. Indeed, these three distinct activities dominate what people do in organizations.

Winning and Developing Resources

Some examples are obvious: Salespeople win customers, product development people develop products, fund-raisers bring in cash, accounts departments make sure that cash is received from those who owe you money. But people have a more extensive role in building the organization's resources.

- **They develop potential resources outside the organization.** Marketing people, for example, may not directly win customers—that is what salespeople do—but they create potential customers who understand and relate to your products and services, making it possible for salespeople to do their job.
- **They develop resources within the organization.** Development engineers take crude prototypes and develop them into real products that work reliably and can be produced profitably.
- **They develop "soft" or intangible resources.** Trainers develop skills in others.

Retaining Resources

Salespeople again provide a good example. Having won customers, they have to spend time keeping those customers happy so that they stay with you. If you have too few salespeople, customers may lose interest or be seduced by your competitors, and you will start to lose them.

On the same principle, accounting staff make sure cash does not leak out of the organization, product development people make sure your product range does not get out of date, and marketing people ensure sufficient advertising and promotional activity to keep potential customers aware. In charities, fund-raising departments keep donors from losing interest, and hospitals' medical specialists ensure that doctors continue to refer patients to their institution.

Using Resources

Having built and retained the resources that make up your enterprise, people then decide what to do with them and how to derive the greatest benefit from them. Salespeople work to get customers to buy more, finance staff make sure that cash is put to best use, product developers try to improve products' functionality, and production staff work to increase plant productivity. In the voluntary sector, people try to stimulate more contributions from donors; in politics, campaigners try to develop active supporters.

People carry out other activities, of course, such as keeping production lines and services running. But the three activities above account for most of what people do to develop and sustain a business.

A Special Case: Human Resource Professionals

The strategic management of people is an extensive topic with numerous dimensions (Schuler & Jackson, 2007). When it comes to managing an organization's resources though, human resource (HR) professionals are indeed special in a number of ways:

- The resources for which they have responsibility are the other people in the organization.
- The HR function clearly has some responsibility for *winning* the people that the organization needs. This involves more than just the obvious tasks of placing job advertisements and arranging interviews. It also entails "marketing" the organization to potential employees and the outside world, setting the "price" it will offer (salary and benefits), and "selling" the organization to potential applicants.
- HR personnel are also involved in *developing* other people, for example, by meeting training and development needs and identifying career opportunities.
- The HR team plays a role in *retaining* an organization's people, for example, by ensuring that terms and conditions remain competitive or working with line management to maintain motivation.

- Most importantly, HR is different because it has much less direct control over the processes involved than other functions do. With the exception of a few mundane tasks, almost all the influence that HR personnel have on the organization's people must be exerted *through other people*. Line managers are, of course, a dominant influence on employees' behavior: They determine how each person is deployed, developed, motivated, and so on. However, individuals respond to influences from many other sources as well: colleagues, senior management, subordinates. Even outsiders can have an impact on your staff—customers who are appreciative of what is done for them build your staff's motivation, while aggressive or offensive customers, such as some call-center staff have to contend with, can damage their morale to the point that they leave.

If HR professionals are to understand their contribution to delivering the organization's performance, then they need tools that clarify the connection between people and results and explain what drives these changes. This clarity will highlight the levers that are available for developing their organization's people resources in ways that will improve future performance—a truly *strategic* view of HR policy.

Case Example

The Role of People in Directing Performance: Starbucks

The fast food industry may be noted for its ability to get unskilled people up to speed so quickly that they can become effective almost immediately and develop rapidly through supervisory and management levels. It is perhaps not so admired for success in retaining people—staff satisfaction ratings of 50%–60% are common, and staff turnover can hit 300% per year! No wonder people need to be productive fast.

Starbucks turned this industry norm on its head, devoting considerable effort to staff satisfaction and retention in the belief that this was essential to retaining customers and winning their spending. From the start, generous health insurance and stock options for even the newest employees—referred to, by the way, as "partners"—helped push satisfaction levels to more than 80%. Starbucks hit second place among large U.S. companies in the *Fortune* 2005 ranking of best places to work. The direct result of this success was turnover rates way below industry averages at 70%–80% per year.

It is when these advantages impacted on customers, though, that the real benefits showed up. Staff who stay around get to know their customers, and this helped visits to the company's stores become a regular part of their lives. And it is not just direct employee benefits that get attention—the company spends more on employee training and development than on marketing. As CEO David Pace remarked in an interview with *Workforce Management* (Weber, 2005), "We're not giving these benefits to our employees because we're a successful company. We're successful because we're giving to our people. We believe it's a fundamental way to run our business. We're in business and we need to deliver to our shareholders. The difficult decision is, Do I spend money and risk profitability, or do I make cuts? We go with what's best for the long-term health of the organization . . . we round on the side of the partner."

It is not hard to work out some back-of-envelope impression of just what all this is worth. The most loyal consumers visited their local store 18 times each month—nearly twice for every working day of the month. If service quality had been less exceptional and customer usage had been only two-thirds of this frequency, then the company's revenue would not have been $9 billion in 2007 but only $6 billion. But then, with lower customer usage, many of the stores that have been opened over the years would never have been viable. So instead of the 15,000 outlets operating at the end of 2007, it would have been operating many fewer, and revenue would have been considerably less than that $6 billion.

Think too about the impact on hiring and training itself. With 170,000 employees, 80% turnover means hiring and training more than 130,000 new people each year. If turnover were a more typical 200% each year, that hiring rate would increase to 340,000 people per year. And that is in addition to the need to find some 30,000 extra people each year to staff their newly opened stores, often in new geographic markets. A further advantage arising from strong staff retention, then, is that it "breeds" people with experience who become available to support the opening of new stores.

But even leaders in HR strategy and practice find it hard to keep the wheels on the track. The company has sometimes struggled to sustain sales growth in established stores, and profit margins fell back after 2005. It has to be remembered, though, that the company's aggressive strategy of market saturation has meant flooding localities with more and more outlets, effectively cannibalizing its own business. Nor is it always possible to keep staff as happy as the leadership would like. As one employee remarked in March 2007, "In the past several years there has been almost no internal promotion; the prevalence of external hiring coupled with high turnover means that almost no-one above the rank of store manager is actually familiar with what Starbucks corporate culture and values are supposed to look like, or how a store runs" (ShiftyStuporvisor, 2007). Nevertheless, many companies in many industries would be thankful indeed to enjoy the kind of people power that Starbucks has built and sustained over many years.

Action Checklist

How Much Impact Do Your People Have on Growing Other Resources in Your Organization?

Most organizations share a few simple types of resources: customers (or other clients if you are in a not-for-profit sector), products or services, physical capacity, and staff.

- What quantity of each of these resources do you have, and how quickly do you need them to grow?
- How much difference would it make to your ability to grow these resources, including staff themselves, if you had 10% more people, or people with 10% more experience?

- How much difference would these same improvements then make to your sales and profits or other performance aims?
- To what extent do you compromise what you would *really* like to have in terms of numbers of people and the investment in rewarding them and training them so you can satisfy investors or others looking for short-term results?

CHAPTER 2

Understanding Staff Dynamics

Overview

This chapter explains a crucial characteristic that your pool of people shares with all other resources: It fills up and drains away over time, like water in a bathtub. This characteristic is vitally important to the way things change through time and has effects on performance that can be difficult to understand and manage. This chapter explains the following:

- **what an "accumulating resource" like staff actually is**, and how such items behave over time, with examples of staffing dynamics
- **how this concept can be extended to understand the development of people through several stages** and the management challenges this can create

Accumulating Resources

Like cash, customers, products, and all other resources, people accumulate over time. The number of people you have today is not "explained" by salaries, work pressures, motivation, or anything else; it is *precisely* the total of everyone you have ever hired minus all those you have ever lost. This is not an opinion, a theory, or a statistical observation. It is an unavoidable law of nature. So tough has this challenge of winning and retaining people become in some industries that it has been named "the war for talent" (Michaels, Handfield-Jones, & Axelrod, 2001). While use of the term is often focused on staff groups with especially rare and valuable skills, winning and retaining staff of all kinds can be a major issue, as the fast-food industry example in chapter 1 illustrates.

The basic principle is captured in Exhibit 2.1. The tank in the middle holds the number of staff you have right now. To the left is the outside world, where there are many people, some of whom might become future employees. The big "pipe" connected to the tank has a pump that drives the speed at which people flow into the tank to join the pool of staff. On the right, another pump on a pipe leading out of the tank determines how fast you lose staff, and again you can see people in the outside world who include our former employees. Since the tank contains what is effectively the inventory or "stock" of staff, and the pipes and pumps depict the rate at which people "flow" into and out of that stock, this structure is commonly referred to as the "stock and flow" framework.

To understand how this works in practice, imagine you are experiencing a high resignation rate in one department, leading to a shortage of staff. In response, you advertise to fill the shortfall. In the meantime, however, your existing staff are overworked and demoralized, so you suffer further resignations. The number of staff will have filled up somewhat, but then drained away back to an even lower level.

Exhibit 2.2 shows what happens to the number of staff during a year of changes. The firm starts with 100 people, but your hiring rate of 10 per month is insufficient to replace the 20 per month that are leaving. Work pressure increases, so you lose 25 people in February and 30 in March. By April, you have increased hiring to match the high rate of attrition. The remaining staff are relieved and encouraged to see that you are fixing the problem, so resignation rates start to decrease. By August, losses are down to 10 people per month, but you keep hiring at 30 per month for August and September to build up the larger number of staff you

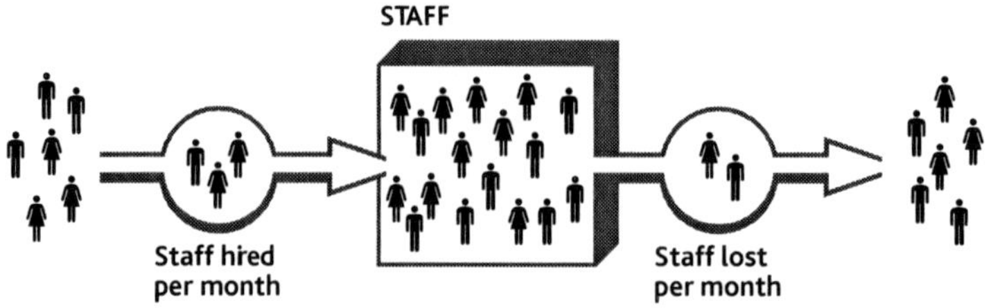

Exhibit 2.1. Building and Losing Staff

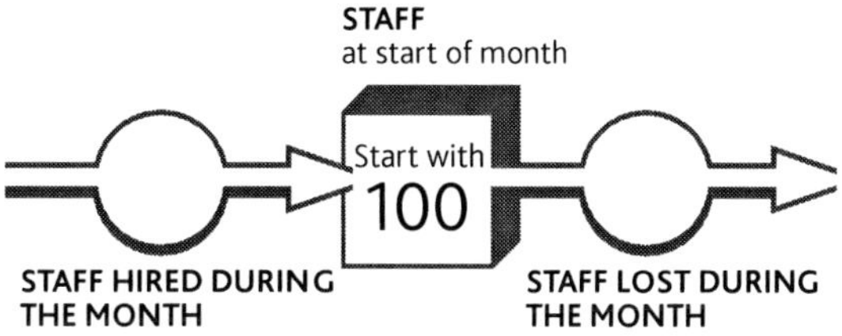

January	**10**	**100**	**20**
February	10	90	25
March	10	75	30
April	30	55	30
May	30	55	25
June	30	60	20
July	30	70	15
August	30	85	10
September	30	105	10
October	10	125	10
November	10	125	10
December	10	125	10
End of December		**125**	

Exhibit 2.2. Working Out Growth and Loss of Staff Through Time

originally needed. You end the year hiring at the lower rate of 10 per month, which matches the attrition rate, and you at last have a stable staff group.

These monthly numbers can readily be shown in the form of time charts such as Exhibit 2.3. We retain the image of the bathtub or tank of staff, with the pipes and pumps showing the rate at which people are flowing in and out.

It is important to note that Exhibits 2.2 and 2.3 label the flows entering the staff resource as "Staff hired (or lost) *during the month*," and this is *always* the relationship between resources and the flows that fill or drain them. Whatever the resource in the tank, the flows are always measured

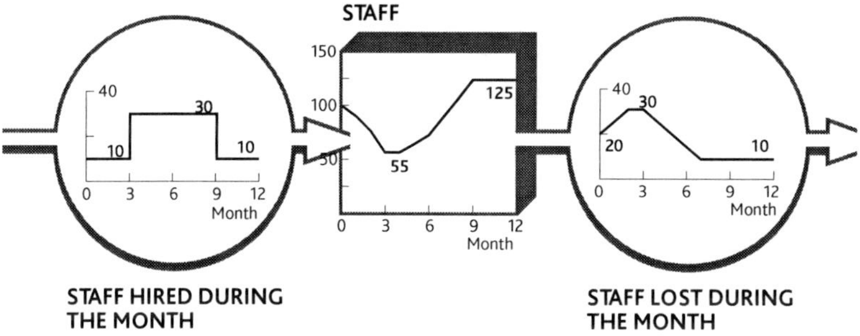

Exhibit 2.3. The Change in Staff Numbers Over Time

in units of "resource per time period." **There is never any exception to this rule.**

Time charts reveal why managing resources through time is harder than we might imagine. It is not at all obvious, if we look at the *inflows and outflows* of staff, why the current *stock* of staff follows the time path that it does. Only when the rates of gain and loss are equal is the head-count stable, for example, in April to May and October to December. When the *net* flow is constant, the stock of staff is changing at a constant rate. For example, in August to September, there is a net inflow of 20 per month, so the chart of staff numbers is rising in a straight line.

Exhibit 2.3 is a typical example of an extremely common structure known as the stock and flow framework. This mechanism is fundamental to how businesses, other organizations, and many other kinds of systems behave over time and lies at the heart of a rigorous method for mapping and modeling performance—system dynamics (Forrester, 1961; Sterman, 2000). The frameworks in this book are entirely consistent with this method.

Doing It Right

The Importance of Numbers

This idea of resources filling and draining seems simple; after all, such things are going on around us all the time, from the real water in a real bathtub to the cash in our bank or visitors to an amusement park. However, merely knowing that this process is happening is not enough. If we want to take control of our situation, we need to know the following:

- how many staff there are
- how quickly the numbers of staff are changing
- how strongly these flows of people are influenced by things under our control and by other forces

And remember that the same principles apply to customers, product ranges, and other resources.

Case Example

Lessons From the War for Talent in the Technology Sector

The apparently simple relationship between resources and their rates of change can cause big problems. In May 2001, the business press carried highly critical articles about the redundancy programs at major technology firms such as Lucent, Nortel, and Ericsson. The articles were not so much concerned with the need to downsize in itself; that had become unavoidable after the disastrous downturn in the sector. The real complaint was that, just months after they had declared major redundancies, firms were announcing *further* rounds of layoffs that were often larger than the first cuts.

This situation arose because of the unrealistic expectation that the rapid expansion of the late 1990s would continue. With business growth often exceeding 20% per year, staffing requirements in sales, customer support, and other functions had skyrocketed. On top of this growing need, firms had to cope with high rates of staff turnover as a vicious war for talent tempted staff to move from firm to firm. Annual attrition rates of 25%–40% were common. Taken together, the growth requirements and turnover meant that departments could be hiring as many *new* staff each year as the number they started with! Although it was never realistic to assume that this boom would continue forever, many firms were nevertheless taken by surprise when business turned down during 2000. It took a few months to realize just how severe the collapse in business activity was going to be, by which time staff numbers had grown well beyond what was needed.

Naturally, hiring rates were slashed, and redundancies were worked out in order to bring staffing back to the lower levels required. In estimating the layoffs that would be needed, companies allowed for natural attrition. Unfortunately many assumed that the previous high staff turnover rates would continue. However, the rapid drop in job security led many staff to stay, so that turnover dropped sharply, often to as little as 5%–8% per annum. That is why companies had to revise their estimates and go through a second round of layoffs.

Sadly, the hiring and firing error in these technology and e-commerce companies also afflicted the consulting firms who advised them. In some cases, the estimation error was compounded by a further failure to think ahead.

During the most frenetic period in the war for talent, these consulting firms were also experiencing unprecedented rates of staff turnover as their best staff left to make themselves rich in the new economy. In a desperate effort to keep servicing the continuing rapid growth they expected, many firms made a special deal with departing consultants: If their new career did not work out, then the consulting firms would guarantee them a return position. When did these career plans go wrong and drive the former consultants back to their previous employers? Precisely when they were no longer needed and the consulting firms themselves were struggling to cope with their own downsizing pressures. Amazingly, in spite of the crystal clear lesson this episode provided, some of these firms went through exactly the same error again in the 2008 recession!

Doing It Right

Gains and Losses Are Both *Vital*

This example from the technology sector vividly illustrates how vital it is to track both win rates and loss rates of key resources. Knowing the net flow alone is not enough. Hiring at the rate of 1,000 people per month while losing 500 per month is a very different challenge from hiring 500 per month with no attrition. Hiring and training costs will be considerably higher in the first case, average experience will stall at a low level, and the high proportion of novices will disrupt the smooth working of the teams that they join.

This is true of many other resources as well. For example, there is a world of difference between one mobile phone firm winning 50,000 new customers a month and another that wins 200,000 a month while at the same time losing 150,000. All else being equal, the second business incurs much higher costs for each additional subscriber added, and if these ratios continue for long, the market will contain millions of former subscribers who are unlikely to return.

Thinking Ahead Is Essential—And Possible!

The story of the technology sector has further implications for the way that the mix of skills and experience in these firms changed over the boom and bust period. Many were left with a serious imbalance between staff groups and between different levels of seniority.

It is interesting to reflect on how these leading companies made a seemingly basic error. After all, they are led by some of the sharpest people around. But while hindsight is in plentiful supply, foresight is much scarcer. No one could be sure, for example, when growth would slow, or by how much, or how quickly. Even when activity started to slow, no one could be certain at first that this really *was* a downturn rather than just a temporary pause. Nevertheless, employees and investors could reasonably have expected better strategic management from their top professionals, for several reasons. For one thing, scenario-based approaches to strategy had been well understood since the mid-1980s. And it is top management's

Case Example

Exploring the Future: Royal Dutch/Shell

A dramatic example of the link between people, resources, and performance occurred at Royal Dutch/Shell. In the late 1960s, the company set up a unit, managed by Pierre Wack, to overcome problems of cash flow management and to forecast future cash requirements. When traditional techniques for forecasting cash flow ran into problems, Wack's diagnosis was that it was because they were trying to apply statistical techniques without properly understanding the issues affecting the quantity and quality of each resource, such as demand from customers and the supply of oil.

Wack's team started to discuss the question of what was predictable: in this case, the future of the global oil price and issues of supply and demand. (In the process, he developed and refined an approach that we now recognize as scenario planning.) Demand for oil was assumed to be secure, so the team focused on supply. This was also assumed to be secure, with established price trends seen as being likely to continue.

Wack was not satisfied. He wanted to know if other factors caused uncertainty in the robustness of resources. The team started to list stakeholders and quickly arrived at governments in oil-producing countries. Wack posed the question, would they be happy to continue increasing production year on year? Would this be in their interest? It soon became apparent to Wack that these governments were unlikely to remain amenable to Shell's activities. The overwhelming logic for the oil-producing countries was to reduce supply, raise prices, and conserve their reserves.

When Wack outlined this argument to his superiors, they told him that there was a lack of unity among oil-producing countries and that the oil companies were in control. Wack's response was to continue focusing on resources and sharpening his thinking. Then the scenario became reality. The 1973 Israeli–Arab War had a dramatic impact, with the political embargo limiting the supply of oil. Prices rose fivefold. Fortunately for Shell, Wack's work had encouraged the company to prepare and take strategic action well ahead of the competition. Shell's position in the profitability of oil companies rose from seventh to second place. The economic value Shell derived from understanding its resource system and being well prepared was calculated at billions of dollars.

The point of scenario planning, as the example of Pierre Wack shows, is not to forecast the future but to check that strategy is robust against *plausible* futures. In the technology sector's war for talent, *some* downturn was always inevitable at *some* point in the near future. One senior partner in a consulting firm pointed out in 1999 that if it continued growing its MBA recruitment at the then current rate, it would be hiring every graduate from every business school within 10 years! So it is hardly surprising that the boom could not go on much longer. Exactly the same dynamic repeated in the investment banking industry in the years up to 2008.

job to look over the horizon and prepare for likely developments—both good and bad (de Geus, 1988; van der Heijden, 2005).

In the technology sector case, although the scale and timing of the 2001 downturn could not have been forecast precisely, companies could have estimated some reasonable scenarios. For example, many technology firms were selling equipment in large volumes to newly incorporated customers. It would have been reasonable to work out what demand rates would have been if new business formation rates had fallen back to historic norms.

What about the decrease in staff turnover itself? Senior human resource (HR) executives have as much responsibility for exploring plausible scenarios as the rest of the top team, so they too could and should have posed the question, "If business activity declines and the job market becomes less secure, what might happen to staff attrition rates?" From that question, it would have been straightforward to look for early signs that a reversal *was* starting, and to work out how the business should respond to new turnover rates of less than 10% per year.

Staff Need to Be Developed and Kept in Balance

We have seen how difficult it can be to understand what happens to a single group of people when the rates of inflow and outflow vary through time. This challenge gets even tougher when they move through successive stages—for example, when people are promoted or transferred. This happens to other resources as well: Products move through different stages of research and development, customers progress through stages of awareness and commitment to your products, and so on.

Exhibit 2.4 shows an example of the dynamics of this process for an organization that has become badly out of balance. The cause was its *accumulated history* of undesirable people flows through its internal development chain. Promotion into the senior level has been quite slow, at just 6 people per year. (All staff flows refer to year 5.) However, turnover has been just 3 per year, so the senior ranks have become overcrowded.

Even promoting just 6 experienced staff each year seems to have been too many. But it is not that simple. Promoting this number out of 50, as

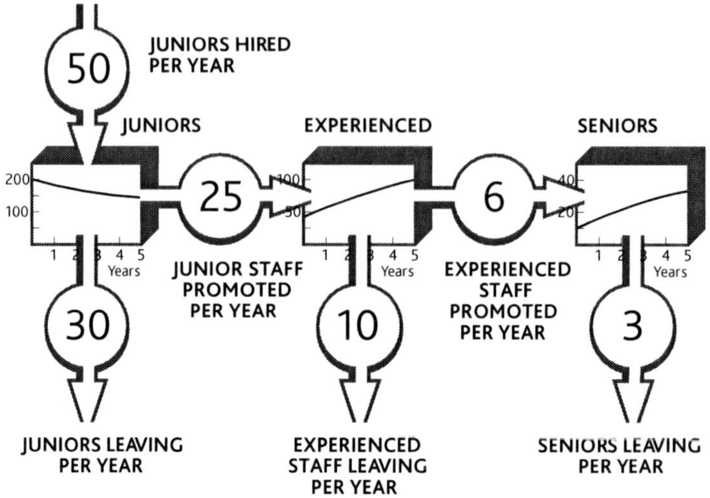

Exhibit 2.4. The Staff Promotion Chain

in year 1, means that experienced people will have to wait more than 8 years for promotion. By the time we get to year 5, the wait has grown to 16 years! So slowing down promotion risks leaving experienced staff frustrated, increasing their resignation rate. Similar observations apply to the promotion of juniors to mid-level jobs. At this point, it is worth reviewing the comment of the Starbucks employee in chapter 1 regarding the lack of promotions among management levels and wondering whether that company too got some of its people-flows wrong.

This example illustrates an important and misunderstood feature of HR systems: the need for balance. Although we might imagine that finding enough good people is the usual challenge, the HR chain can be a management development machine that generates a constant stream of more senior people than your organization can use.

This explains why some professional service firms operate a policy of "up or out." After spending a few years in one grade, every professional is expected to either seek promotion or leave. At first sight, this policy may seem bizarre. Why would an organization deliberately remove people who may be doing a fine job where they are? The answer is to make space for lower grades, keeping open the opportunity for advancement and the motivation that flows from it.

Long-Run Shortages Must Be Managed

Not every organization enjoys such an embarrassment of riches, however. One pension fund firm was worrying about its ability to maintain the spectacular growth of the previous decade. It feared that an era of rapid industry growth was giving way to market saturation. Even worse, its success had attracted many competitors to the industry, and profit margins were falling fast. The firm's share price reflected its strong track record, so continued growth was important. Without it, the commitment of senior investment professionals whose rewards were linked to the share price would collapse. These skilled professionals were vital to the firm's success. If they left, its reputation would be destroyed, so setting in motion a vicious cycle of decline.

After carefully considering the market conditions that the company faced, management checked to see whether there were enough people to continue its development. The result is shown in Exhibit 2.5.

This HR structure looks rather unusual. Many firms have a pyramid structure; this organization has an *inverted* pyramid, with nearly as many directors as all the other professional grades combined. These top people are managing huge sums of money, and the business relies on them for its extremely critical investment decisions. Moreover, the tight profit margins in fund management make it costly to employ junior people who are

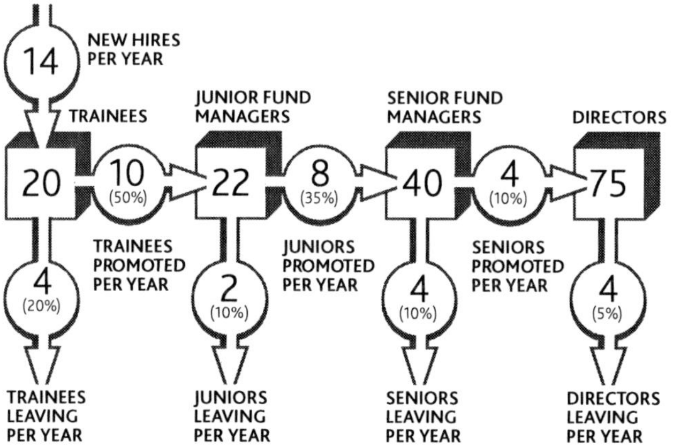

Exhibit 2.5. Fund Management Staff Structure

not contributing to the firm's performance (Doman, Glucksman, Tu, & Warren, 2000).

Note that in the situation shown here, the rate at which people are *entering* each grade exactly matches the rate at which they are *leaving*: 14 new trainees are hired at the same time as 10 are promoted and 4 quit. This organization is frozen in scale and structure.

Given that the firm needed to grow, it faced a dilemma. Even allowing for improved productivity, the most senior groups would still need to grow by 10% per year. This meant, for example, that another eight people would need to be promoted to director each year—three times the present rate! Where would these extra people come from? The senior grade is too small to provide a sufficient flow of people with enough experience; there are shortages in the outside world; and if outsiders *were* brought in, they would probably disrupt the strong culture that currently existed within the business.

The situation is insoluble, which explains why the firm sold itself to a major international investment bank within a year of making this analysis. The new owner had the opposite problem: plenty of ambitious young people with not enough opportunity for development.

Case Example

Developing Cross-Cultural Talent at HSBC

Every year, the financial services giant HSBC sends bright graduates and managers into long-term business experiences abroad, thereby building a cohort of international officers. Locations include western countries as well as transitional economies as far apart as Saudi Arabia, Indonesia, and Mexico. Any manager who expects to make a career at HSBC must pay their dues on these kinds of international missions, following in the footsteps of the chairman, Sir John Bond, and other top executives. In this way, HSBC continuously develops a global cohort of young managers capable of surmounting barriers to cross-border learning. Similar approaches are pursued by other multinationals to enable them to transfer expertise and know-how across geographical, cultural, and political divides.

Changing the Staff Mix

The linear development of people from one state to another is not always sufficient to achieve the staffing changes you require. A common challenge comes when changes need to be made to the *mix* of staff types.

One traditional mining firm was trying to move from a long-standing "command and control" culture toward an organization in which initiative and self-reliance would be the norm. The transition involved many subtleties to do with changes in rewards, leadership, style, and culture, but at its core lay a need to reduce the number of people exhibiting old behaviors and increase the number adopting the new style. The firm embarked on a coaching program to upgrade the capabilities of its existing managers and at the same time set out to hire people who already had the capabilities it needed.

The firm originally thought it could achieve the change by coaching a large proportion of existing staff and hiring new people at a fairly modest rate. On working through the numbers, however, it discovered that the more rapid turnover among these new managers would prevent it from reaching its target number of people. Consequently a very rapid coaching rate would be required for existing staff, and the hiring of new management also had to be far more rapid than had previously been thought necessary (Exhibit 2.6).

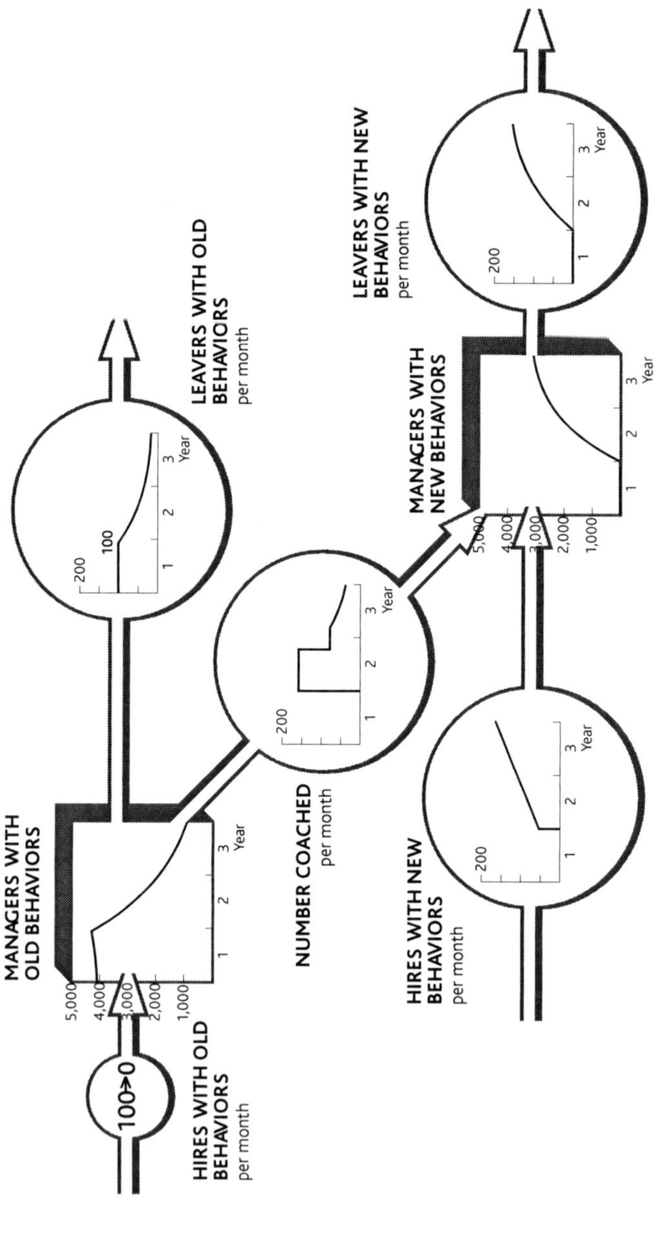

Exhibit 2.6. Rapid Coaching and Recruitment of Managers With New Behaviors

Action Checklist

Using the Numbers

Qualitative discussions about how staff numbers develop and how to direct them into the future are not adequate. If you want to work out what to do and when, there is no escaping the need to work out the numbers. This involves the following steps:

- To understand your organization's path through time, you must **start with time charts** like those in Exhibits 2.3 and 2.4. Snapshot numbers, as used in Exhibit 2.5, are not sufficient, because not only are the *stocks* of people in each state changing, but so too are the *flows* between those stocks.
- Next, **to work out what is happening you need the data.** Firms often seem to know little about how their key resources are changing. That applies not just to people, but to customers, product ranges, dealers, and others.
- **You cannot "guesstimate" the figures.** Even people who have used this method for years cannot look at resource flows such as Exhibit 2.3 and sketch accurately what will happen to the stock of staff. It is just plain hard to do! There is no choice but to work it out, as shown in Exhibit 2.2.
- **Look for explanations in the historic information.** Use this evidence to clarify why staff movements have taken place at the rate they have. The future may well reflect additional factors or different influences, of course, but do not ignore learning that could be important.
- Look to the future and **project what you want to see happen to your numbers.** Then work through the flow rates of people that would have to occur to bring about the future path you want. Check that the drivers of these flows (including those outside your control) are plausible, and ask yourself how much these numbers could vary if events turn out to be different from what you expect. A great question to keep

in mind throughout is "What is the worst thing that could happen in this situation?" This is followed of course by "Can I prevent or mitigate it?" and if not, "Can I prepare the organization to cope with it?"

CHAPTER 3

Resource Interdependence

Overview

As we saw in chapter 1, people are essential to an organization's performance because of their influence over winning, developing, sustaining, and utilizing the resources that make up the enterprise. This chapter will do the following:

- **explore the interdependence of resources, and in particular,** how they combine to assemble the "strategic architecture" of the enterprise
- **highlight the impact people have** on these interdependencies
- **explain the significance of people as custodians of resources** in managing the wider system

The Interdependence of Resources

If human resource (HR) professionals are to help the management team improve performance, they need to appreciate how the business system actually functions to deliver that performance. The essentials of this understanding are as follows:

- **Current performance depends on current stocks of resources.** Customers drive revenues, for example, and staff and capacity drive costs.
- **All resources accumulate and drain away through time.** Indeed, this is the defining characteristic of resources. They also develop from stage to stage. It is the *flows* of resources into, through, and out of the business that determine how the levels of each change through time.

- **The only way in which performance can change (in a stable environment) is if we win or lose resources through time.** If resources do not flow, then the quantity of their current stock does not change. Rather obviously, if you do not gain or lose staff, the *number* of people remains constant. The same is again true of all resources.

So the critical question we are left with is "What drives resources to flow into and out of a business and develop from stage to stage?" The answer is simple: **The rate at which every resource fills and drains away depends, unavoidably, on *existing* resource levels.** Your customer win rate reflects the number of salespeople you have, and your product development rate reflects the cash and people you devote to the task.

These dependencies are not always linear; there will come a point at which adding more people to either of these two tasks ceases to be effective. Resource flow rates may also be driven by intangible factors such as staff skills and product performance. But the fundamental point is inescapable: The rate at which resources are changing *always* reflects the stocks of resource that are already present.

Understanding Resource Flows

We can illustrate this point with some examples from the HR field. The rate at which you can hire new people depends on the number of people available to undertake the hiring effort: writing job descriptions, placing advertisements, screening applications, conducting first interviews, and so on. Similarly the rate at which you can train people depends on the numbers of trainers available.

This highlights several important points about resource flows:

- **Resources do not have to be "owned" to be available to you.** For example, outside trainers you can call on are equally relevant to the rate of training you can achieve.
- **Your success rate may well depend on more than one factor.** Your hiring success, for example, could depend on three distinct resources: the number of people working on the hiring effort,

the *existing* number of staff (e.g., by recommending their friends to join you—or avoid you!), and your reputation among potential recruits. Note that this last item is an intangible factor.

- **Flows that depend on existing resources can be negative as well as positive.** The rates at which people leave, for example, may well reflect work pressure, which can readily arise from having too much work for the current number of employees. If this work is driven by customer demand, staff attrition will reflect the balance between two resources: the number of customers and the number of staff. The more customers there are piling on the work pressure, the faster staff may leave. To compound the problem, the *fewer* staff you have, the faster still more of them will leave.

The Firm's Strategic Architecture

Current resource levels drive the rates at which *all* resources are changing. This is the meaning of interdependence within a firm's set of resources. When these linkages are made explicit, we can see in detail how each piece connects, where it connects, and the strength of that relationship. Once we put all these connections together they generate a complete description of how the enterprise functions, its *strategic architecture*, complete with information about how it is developing through time. The framework we will now develop is related to—but more precise and rigorous than—the strategy maps that some companies assemble for the purpose of planning and directing their business (Kaplan & Norton, 2004).

Example: The Professional Service Firm

We can illustrate the idea of a strategic architecture by looking at how one kind of business functions. Although you may not work in a professional firm yourself, or be particularly familiar with such organizations, it is nevertheless a useful example because similar structures often apply to important groups within other types of organizations. Many information technology (IT) departments, for example, have to develop skilled professionals to fulfill their roles and operate by taking on work for "clients" in other parts of the organization.

For professional service firms, clients provide the demand for which the organization gets paid. Often this demand comes in the form of distinct projects. In the example that we will consider, clients have sufficiently frequent needs that they can become loyal users of the firm's services.

Exhibit 3.1 shows how the client base develops during the early years. Clients must be won and retained. Our story concerns a firm that initially provides attractive services that offer good value. By the end of year 1, clients are being won very quickly, as we can see from the high value of the "Clients won per year" chart and the steep slope of the "Clients" resource itself. By the middle of year 2, the firm's staff can no longer cope with the many projects demanded by this large number of clients. The quality of work declines, mistakes are made, and projects are not finished on time, so clients start to leave. At the same time, the firm finds it harder to win new clients. This at least slows the mounting pressure on staff, giving them the chance to cope with the workload.

On the staff side, our firm starts with a small group of trained professionals and a very small number of trainees (Exhibit 3.2). However, it hires at a rapid rate and operates a fast apprenticeship system, allowing the group of skilled professionals to grow quickly. Even so, by the middle of year 2, project workloads are so high that these key staff are overloaded. The pressure becomes intolerable for many of them, and resignation rates rise. Fortunately the slower growth in clients and projects eases the pressure, so that over years 3 and 4 the turnover among professional staff gradually declines.

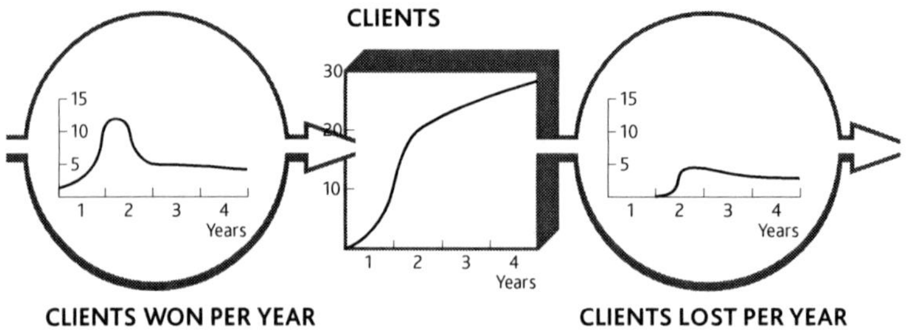

Exhibit 3.1. Client Development for a Professional Service Firm

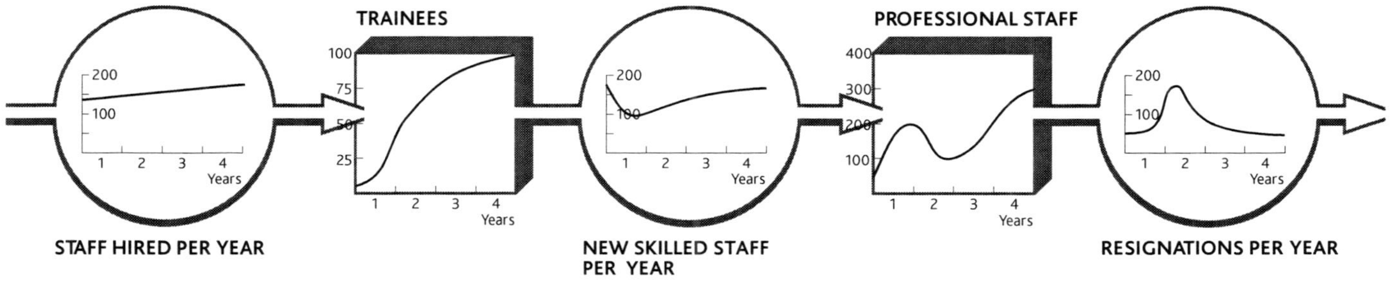

Exhibit 3.2. Staff Development for a Professional Firm

The way the firm makes money is simple: It receives fees for project work and incurs costs largely made up of the salaries of its professional staff. There are also other costs, of course, such as office space, administrative systems, and support staff. Exhibit 3.3 shows how the firm's profits develop over time, shaped by the history of clients and staff numbers.

The last piece of the architecture to consider consists of the interactions between clients, projects, and staff. The rate at which resources change depends on the resources already in place. This interdependence can drive growth, constrain growth, and drive resource losses.

- The large number of staff in year 1 allows the firm to win clients rapidly.
- The limited staff capacity in year 2 slows the client acquisition rate.

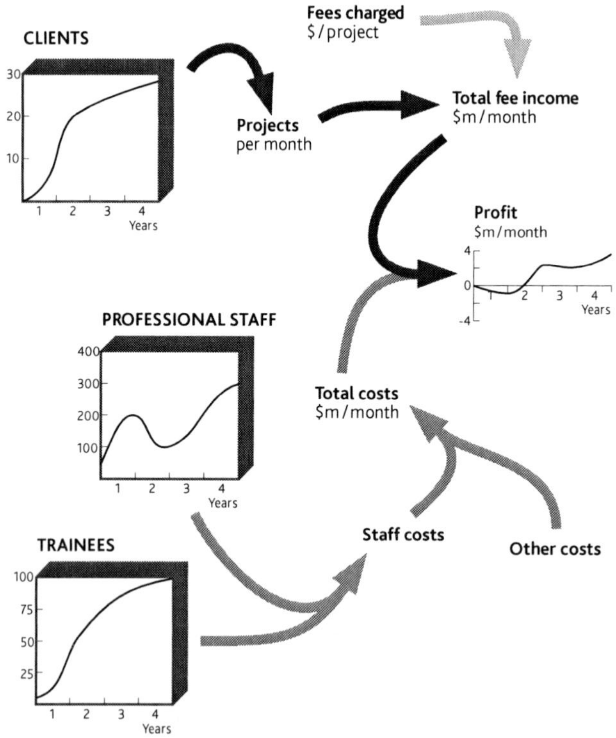

Exhibit 3.3. How a Professional Firm Makes Money

- Finally, the excess of clients in relation to staff triggers losses of both clients and staff.

If we connect these pieces together, we get a strategic architecture for our professional firm (Exhibit 3.4). At first sight this may look rather daunting, but if you follow the story around the picture, you should be able to understand what each link means. Just stick to the rule that a curved arrow means "If I know *X*, I can calculate or estimate *Y*." If you know the project workload and the work capacity of your staff, for example, then you can calculate "Pressure on staff." If you know the staff pressure, then you can estimate "Quality of work" (such as error rates or deadlines missed), and hence work out the rate at which you lose clients. "Pressure on staff" also determines the rate of resignations you can expect.

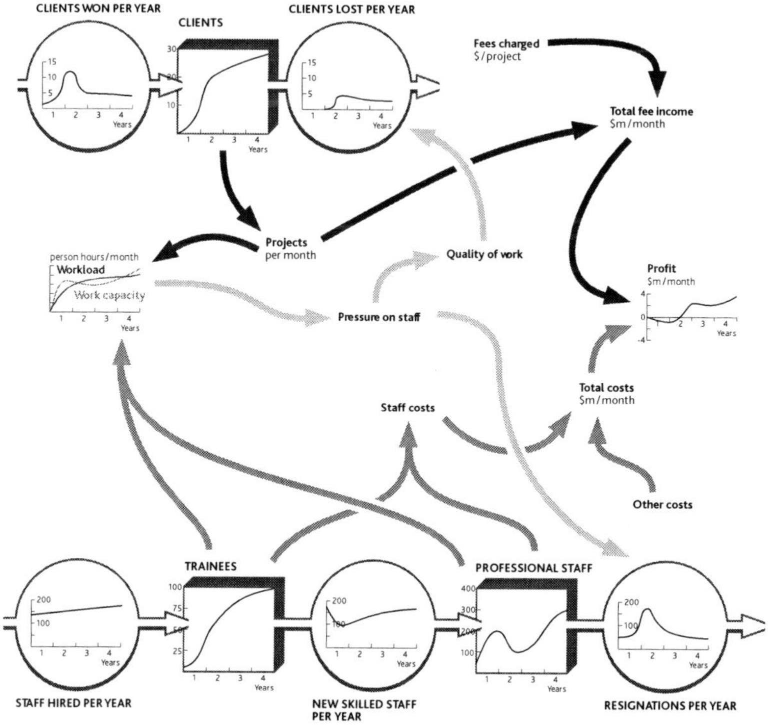

Exhibit 3.4. The Strategic Architecture for a Professional Firm

Doing It Right

Understand the Drivers of Demand

For our professional service firm, we have seen that projects are largely driven by demand from the *stock* of repeat clients. In markets for consumables, this dominance by the customer stock can be still more pronounced. Demand for Starbucks coffee, for example, is heavily dominated by the stock of current users; first-time users account for a tiny fraction of sales. The same would hold true for, say, voluntary organizations serving the homeless, where it is the accumulated number of homeless people that sets demand for support services.

Where the product or service is a durable or one-off purchase, it is the *inflow rate* of customers that drives demand. The stock of customers is best described as the "installed base." Sales of washing machines, for example, arise only on those very few occasions when people make a one-time purchase. Suppliers of wedding dresses face a similar situation, as do providers of certain services, such as estate agents or immigration advisors. All these organizations only receive "demand" on rare occasions in each customer's or client's life. This does not, of course, make the installed base of past buyers irrelevant; on the contrary, they may exert a strong influence by encouraging or discouraging other people to emulate their choice.

Managing large professional firms, such as KPMG and PWC, with very demanding clients *and* staff, is far from easy (Maister, 2003), but a few provide some of the best examples of a culture dedicated to winning new business from existing clients. These firms have built on their strong relationships with executives, often based originally on mundane audit services, to become powerful financial advisers, systems integrators, and strategy consultants. Although we tend not to think of firms of accountants as customer focused, more of their employees spend more time in customer contact than is the case in almost any other business. It is estimated that of their available working time, 75% is spent directly working with or selling to actual or potential customers.

The Value of a Strategic Architecture

The strategic architecture diagram in Exhibit 3.4 is necessarily simplified and leaves out some connections. It does not, for example, identify separately the most senior group of professionals—the partners who win new clients, lead projects, hire new staff, and so on. Nevertheless, the diagram explains three important items:

1. How performance depends on current resources
2. How resources fill and drain through time
3. How these resources depend on each other to develop

Similar diagrams can be put together for any kind of organization, and organizations in similar sectors tend to share very similar structures. All airlines, for example, have customers, aircraft, routes, and staff, which depend on each other in largely the same way, though, of course, the numbers will vary enormously from case to case. Retail companies like Starbucks (discussed in chapter 1) have stores, staff, a product range, and consumers, and firms in that sector too will share a very similar architecture.

Once you understand this core architecture, further developments become possible:

- You can evaluate **the availability of potential resources that are essential to your growth**, such as skilled staff who it may be possible to hire.
- You can assess **the way that important attributes of resources (such as staff experience) are changing.**
- You can get a better grasp of **intangible factors and their impact**, such as the reputation resource that affects your ability to win customers.
- You can gain a better insight into **rivalry for customers, staff, and other scarce resources.**

This awareness will transform your understanding of *why* performance has followed its past trajectory, and *what you can do* about each important element in your strategy to improve things in the future. Later chapters will explain this in more detail.

The Impact of People

We now have a picture of our firm's resources, their interdependencies, and the link to performance outcomes: our strategic architecture. So where do people fit in? They feature in two vital ways:

1. **Some groups of people are themselves a core resource of the business system**, providing essential capacity for the organization to get things done. If these people are removed, the business will instantly cease to provide its product or service. In a professional service firm of lawyers or accountants, the skilled professionals actually *are* the firm's production capacity. The same is true of staff in consumer service organizations such as restaurants, hairdressers, schools, and the performing arts. In the health sector, doctors and nurses make up most of the capacity to deliver health care.
2. **Other groups of people are custodians of core resources.** If these people are absent, the business will continue to provide its product or service but will gradually start to wind down. For example, product development personnel enhance a firm's product range, but if they are absent the original products will still exist. Marketing people develop aware customers, and that resource will continue to exist for some time before draining away. IT staff build and maintain the information systems on which the organization relies, but if they are not there, existing systems will continue to be available. Salespeople win and retain customers, but if they do not show up for work next Monday, most businesses could continue to rely on customers to place orders.

This is not a completely hard and fast distinction; for example, many sales organizations both win and retain customers *and* capture orders. Conversely, some sales groups have no direct responsibility for customer acquisition at all and purely capture orders. Nevertheless, this distinction between groups who *are* a core resource and others who are *custodians* of core resources helps clarify where people fit in the business system.

Example: Resource Custodians in a Restaurant Business

The professional service example we discussed earlier in this chapter is a clear case where staff (the professionals) are themselves a core resource of the system. To clarify how people are involved when they are *custodians* of core resources, let us think about a restaurant chain such as McDonalds or Pizza Hut. We already mentioned that a large group of staff—those who prepare the food and serve customers—actually constitute the capacity of the business. But there are other groups of people too.

First, we need to identify the core resources and how they are connected. Such businesses rely for most of their revenue on large numbers of regular customers, the major demand-side resource. Occasionally consumers who do not normally visit buy on impulse, but these provide a relatively small fraction of revenue. The supply-side resources include the restaurants themselves, the product range, and service staff. Restaurants give access to new customers. The product range appeals to potential new consumers, but also keeps existing consumers loyal.

We are simplifying this picture for the sake of clarity. In reality, restaurant staff have various roles and grades, each restaurant provides a certain seating capacity, the product range will have items removed as well as added, and so on. However, the core architecture outlined in Exhibit 3.5 is enough to illustrate the custodian roles that staff groups perform in this business.

- There will be product development people experimenting with possible new menu items.
- The marketing team will research customer numbers and usage patterns, and develop and commission advertising campaigns. Here, we are showing only that they work to *win* customers and *keep* them (i.e., encourage them not to leave). In reality, their task is rather more complex, as they need to move consumers through a series of stages, from simple awareness of the firm's product offering through to being loyal users.
- Several groups are involved in developing the firm's stores, seeking new sites, acquiring the real estate, briefing and managing designers and developers, and so on.
- HR staff, plus various line managers, are involved in hiring, training, and trying to retain the service staff required.

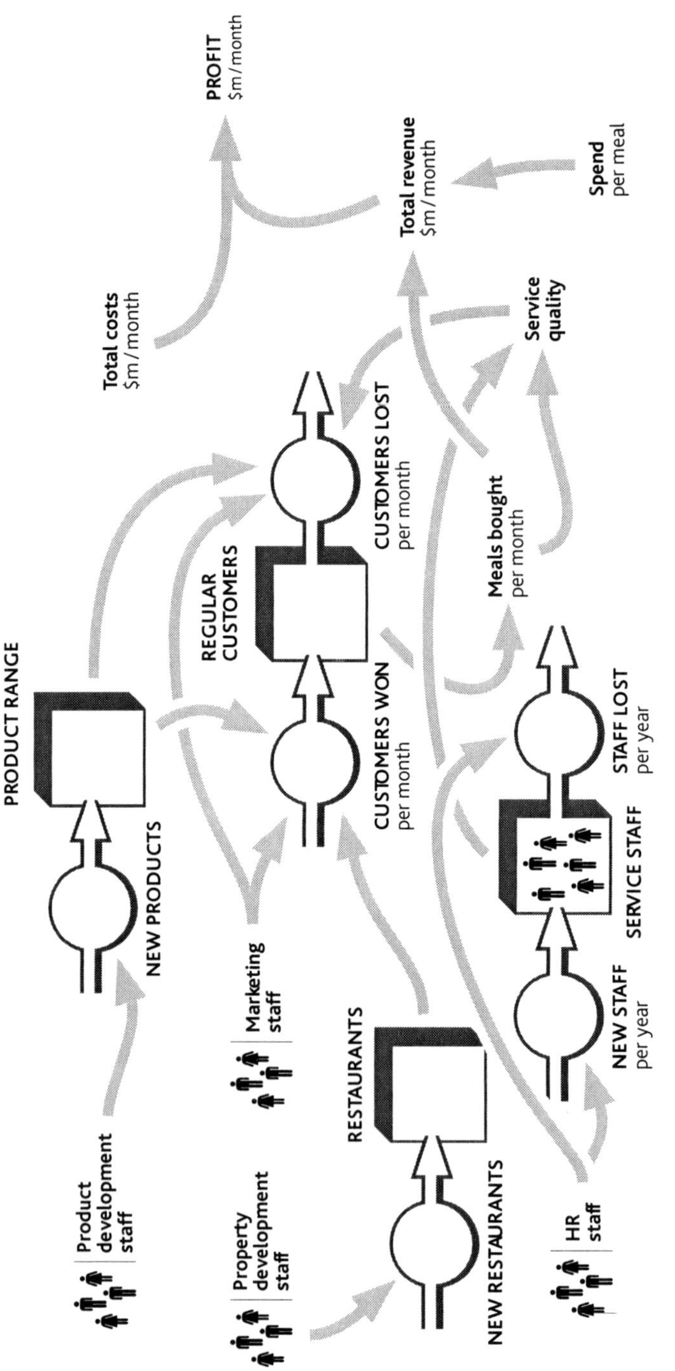

Exhibit 3.5. Staff Groups Develop and Sustain Business Resources for a Restaurant Business

How Groups Act as Custodians of Resources

There are three important observations about the way groups fulfill their roles as custodians of the organization's other resources.

Retaining resources matters as much as winning them. First, it is just as important to pay attention to *retaining* resources as it is to worry about capturing and developing them. Marketing executives, for example, should be paying just as much attention to consumers *leaving* the loyal user group as they do to winning new consumers in the first place. This is not to say that the aim is always retention at any cost. Real estate staff, for example, will have the responsibility of disposing of sites that are no longer wanted or that can be replaced with better units. Product development staff need to constantly review the product range for items that can be removed to make room for more appealing alternatives.

People indirectly affect other resources. Second, although a certain group may have *primary* responsibility for winning, developing, and retaining a specific resource, they may also have an indirect role in relation to resources that other groups look after. Service staff, for example, not only deliver the service directly, but also have a critical role in sustaining the customer base—meaning they try to ensure that people return! Restaurant acquisition staff focus on finding and developing sites but clearly contribute to acquiring customers by ensuring that each outlet is well located and designed. Other operational groups also play resource-sustaining roles. Logistics and delivery staff ensure that products are available, but in so doing they also indirectly contribute to customer retention.

Therefore, it is critical to identify not only which group is *primarily* responsible for winning, developing, or sustaining a resource, but also those other groups that indirectly, or even inadvertently, influence the same flows. Armed with this understanding, teams can put in place procedures to ensure that best use is made of others who can assist them in their goals. Also, teams can ensure that groups who might accidentally undermine valuable efforts both see the danger and avoid it.

HR people have a unique role. The third point to note is the special status of HR staff. One key difference is that much of their activity takes place at another level from the business engine itself: HR staff help to attract and develop the people in other groups who, in turn, win and develop business resources. A major frustration of the HR role is that it is often so difficult to demonstrate its value, to the extent that it is frequently seen simply as a support function. A successful marketing executive can see customers being won quickly; a successful product development person can see the popularity of the products they create; a successful finance function can show how well the organization's spending is controlled; and so on. In contrast, an HR team can point to its *possibly* successful hiring, development, and retention of staff in the belief that these people will ultimately do a good job and vindicate the HR contribution. Even then, managers in other parts of the business will claim, often with good reason, that *they* developed and nurtured these great staff who did so much to deliver performance.

A further important difference is that HR professionals do not necessarily have primary responsibility for winning, developing, and retaining people. That role falls more to the line managers in each function, albeit in partnership with HR staff. The best that HR can do, in many cases, is provide the tools and procedures to enable and encourage line managers to do this well. However, there is evidence that this traditional HR role is broadening, with the best organizations (and the best HR people) increasingly involved in resolving central business issues such as formulating strategy, removing obstacles, and providing opportunities for people to share knowledge and expertise. What makes HR people significant is the often decisive influence they exert on people's effectiveness and ability to acquire, develop, and retain other resources. As we shall see in the next chapter, it is an ability to understand and manage the *attributes* of resources that builds greater effectiveness.

Case Example

Strategic Development at SABMiller

In the early 1990s, South African Breweries (SAB) was a large regional firm, with limited interests in the North American and European markets. Now, through a combination of organic growth and acquisition (notably that of U.S. firm, Miller Brewing), SABMiller is the world's leading brewer in developing markets and the second largest by volume, with 118 breweries in 24 countries. What led SABMiller to achieve this success? How was a decent, if unspectacular, firm able to develop so far, so fast? The answer lies with SABMiller's people, one resource whose development profoundly affected all others.

The first quality they possessed was *awareness*. SABMiller's CEO, Graham McKay, recognized that his company's business position in the apartheid era was, despite many problems, very comfortable. Under this isolated regime, the firm felt protected by tariff barriers and by the reluctance of foreign competition to get involved in what was perceived as a ticking time bomb. As a result, SAB made good profits and employed the best South African managers. However, McKay and his senior colleagues were aware that the situation could not last: The economy was stagnating and challenging commercial realities would soon hit home. According to McKay, SAB customers "were black people who were disenfranchised and were not part of the comfortable commercial round . . . the underlying realities of South African society were much more in our faces than they were of most business managers in South Africa."

Boldness and a capacity to take risks also contributed to the firm's expansion. For Graham McKay, "it comes back to independence of thought, a willingness to look at things fundamentally and say to yourself, what do you really think about this? Where does that come from? What are the fundamental underlying facts, trends, or tendencies?" These attributes enabled SAB's people to go further and faster than many of their contemporaries.

The next reason for SAB's growth was an understanding of the *need to build and concentrate its resources*. This led it to take several challenging initiatives. First, it divested itself of all its nonbrewing businesses, concentrating instead on developing a world-class brewing operation. Second, the firm recognized the need to develop equally high-grade staff capabilities. Because of apartheid, people on production lines were poorly educated and lacked the necessary skills. Therefore the company hired additional temporary staff so that employees could be retrained over a 2-year period. Next, SAB led the way among organizations in South Africa in developing non-white staff into supervisory and managerial positions, a commitment that continues to this day.

Another reason for SAB's rise is linked to some good fortune of timing. The collapse of apartheid coincided with the opening up of overseas markets in China, Latin America, and Central Europe. If apartheid had still been in force, SAB would have been excluded from participating in these markets. McKay views obstacles and handicaps as factors that can be turned to advantage, *embracing change*: "As South Africans, we weren't really frightened of emerging markets compared to the things that we were going through at home."

Strong leadership also characterized SAB's rapid rise. Graham McKay has not courted the publicity and personality cults of many of his contemporaries, and does not believe that success is the result of a single leader. A more cautious CEO would probably have settled for hunkering down and taking the profits; McKay had the vision to change things. His influence is reflected in the culture of his organization, which values personal initiative and seeks to counter complacency.

Through astute development and deployment of formidable resources, attributes, and capabilities, SAB managed to reinvent itself from a regional conglomerate to a global giant. Its challenge since has been to maintain those resources across a broad range of regional businesses that employ many people and face very different situations.

Action Checklist

Understanding Resource Interdependencies and the Strategic Architecture

In this chapter we have seen that resources are unavoidably dependent on each other. The only way to understand exactly how these connections work is to trace what is causing resource flows to run at the speed they do. What is driving customers in or out, staff to join or leave, and so on? When you trace back these dependencies, you will always arrive back at one or more existing resources, either within the organization or outside it. This is the essence of what makes resources complementary.

Here are the steps you need to follow:

- **Develop a chart for the history of each resource** whose growth you want to understand and control.
- **Chart the history of each resource's inflows and outflows.** This will entail investigation and analysis. For example, if you know your historic staff numbers, the change from month to month is the net inflow. If you know the hiring rate, you can work out the loss rate: It is the difference between the hiring rate and the total net staff change. The key variables to explain are the separate inflows and outflows.
- **Trace back to the factors that drive a resource flow and identify how these have changed over the same period.** For example, how many new staff did you try to hire month by month, and how many did you *actually* hire? What accounts for any gap between these? For example, how have you altered your starting salaries relative to your competitors?

Here are the steps you need to follow to deepen your understanding of resource flows and their impact:

- **Use statistical methods** to see if your expected explanations actually do explain the resource flow rate. For example, is customer retention strongly related to the experience of your staff, as we saw for Starbucks in chapter 1?

- **Investigate what might be missing** if your initial list of causes does not seem to explain how resource flows have changed. If you are losing customers in spite of having experienced customer service staff, for example, are your products not good enough, or are competitors pricing more aggressively?

In following the strategic architecture, you will inevitably get back to existing resources, interconnected in a chain of interdependence. For example, staff turnover may be driven by overwork that is caused by having too many customers relative to existing numbers of staff. It is now possible to work around all of these explanations for each resource flow and assess the likely effectiveness of options for managing that flow into the future.

CHAPTER 4

Understanding Resource Attributes

Overview

People differ. In previous chapters we treated all people in a single stock as if they were identical, but a greater level of detail is now required. If we fail to account for these important differences—in skills or experience, say—then we risk making big errors.

What makes individuals different, at least in their contribution to the organization's performance, is certain key attributes that they possess. This applies to other resources as well, such as customer profitability or product functionality, but people are the focus of our attention in this book. This chapter will do the following:

- **explain resource attributes**—what they are, why they are important, and how they change
- **highlight the concept of "coflow**" as the mechanism by which the attributes of resources can be understood, measured, and managed

Resource Attributes

With the notable exception of cash, few resources are identical or uniform. Customers differ widely in their spending power and value to your business, and products differ in the extent to which they appeal to customers. However, when you are managing resources to improve performance, what matters is not simply that resources are different but also the *precise characteristics* on which they differ. Any single resource may carry a number of characteristics that determine how the stock of that resource affects other parts of the system (Warren, 2008, chap. 5). Each of the routes in an airline's network, for example, carries its own unique number of potential passengers, flight distance and flying time, specific airport operating costs, and so on.

Significance of Resource Attributes

Why do resource attributes matter? What makes them so vital to understanding how your organization is performing? They matter for several reasons:

- **The character of each resource changes through time.** If we lose our most effective customer service staff, our levels of service, reputation, and repeat business will suffer faster than if we lost "average" people.
- **The impact that each resource has on others depends on its attributes as well as its quantity.** Exhibit 4.1 offers some measures of attributes that apply in different cases. There may be various possible measures for any attribute, but the best measure is the one that captures how the resource contributes to the rest of the system. Skill level, for example, may in some cases best be measured in terms of numbers of tasks that an individual can do, but in other cases the speed or accuracy with which they work may be better measures.
- **A resource's attributes move with it when it is won or lost.** When people leave, they take their skills and experience with them. When customers are won, they bring with them their demand for your products or services. When new products are introduced, they carry with them some functionality that potential customers may value.
- **Attributes may be potential and latent, rather than actual,** requiring you to put in additional work if you want to realize their benefits. Exhibit 4.1 includes an example of this: potential end customers that are reached by distributors. Distributors are the resource, and adding a new distributor increases the stock of *potential* customers (another resource). However,

Tangible resource	Attributes	Possible attribute measures
Customers	Purchase rate	$/year
Staff	Experience Skill level	Years Fraction of tasks that can be done
Distributors	Market reach	Potential end customers
Products	Potential customer appeal	Functions that each product performs

Exhibit 4.1. Examples of Resource Attributes

these potential customers will only become *active* if we provide products that they want and if our distributors serve and support them effectively.

How Resource Attributes Are Made Up

Few resources consist of individual items that are identical in all respects. A notable exception is cash: Every $1 bill is worth exactly as much as every other one. But such uniformity is rare; individual resource items generally vary.

To help understand this variation within a resource, it is helpful to have a picture of its "quality profile." Consider an organization with too few experienced staff ("experience" in this case simply meaning the number of years in the job). Take the experience of the longest serving person alone, then add to it the experience of the second longest serving, then the third, and so on. If you continue with this process until you have accounted for your entire staff group, you get a curve of cumulative experience versus cumulative staff (Exhibit 4.2).

You can go some way to obtaining this picture by using the "stacked bar chart" feature in your spreadsheet software, shown to the right of Exhibit 4.2, but the distribution curve gives you a much clearer understanding of the situation. It is important to note that Exhibit 4.2, unlike virtually every other diagram in this book, is not a time chart. It is a snapshot analysis of one feature of our people resource right now.

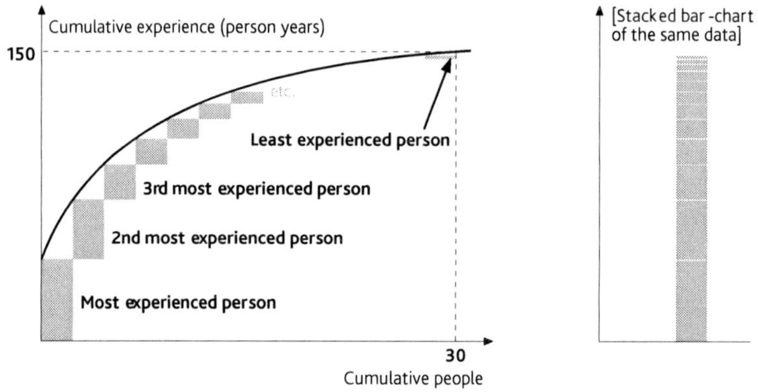

Exhibit 4.2. Experience Profile of a Staff Group

This is not only a mildly interesting picture, but also a practical tool to help you discuss and decide policy. The extent of the "tail" of inexperienced people becomes clear, together with the average level of experience. You can now think about the dynamics that are changing this profile and evaluate your options for altering it toward the shape that you want. For example, if there are no changes at all during the next 12 months, average experience will have grown by 1 year; how far would that go toward giving us the experience we need? What would happen to average experience if our five longest serving people leave, and what critical knowledge would they take with them? How much would we dilute the team's experience if we brought in 20 new people? Answers to these questions depend inescapably on the shape of the curve for your particular case.

Comparable quality profiles exist for resources in other parts of the business. For example, the sales function is concerned with the revenue contribution profile of its customer base, and the distribution department will be looking at the age profile of its vehicles.

This concept is equally important in noncommercial settings. In the voluntary sector, charities need to be aware of the contribution profile of their donors and make conscious choices about where to focus. Should they devote their attention to getting big sums from rich individuals or involve as many contributors as possible, no matter how small?

Before we move on to show how we use resource attributes at a more strategic level, we need to give one important warning, mentioned briefly above: **It is vital to choose the correct attribute for your purpose.** For example, an accountant's *total* work experience, including his work before joining your organization, is more relevant to his job performance than is the number of years he has been with you. Similarly, you may need to be careful about the range of sales performance within a sales team. In the insurance industry, for example, signing up new policies is of little value if most of these policies lapse within the first year or two, so the "sales effectiveness profile" of the sales force might need to track *sustained* policies sold rather than just monthly signups.

You may even need to track more than one attribute. Banks, for example, have a quality mix for the varying sizes of the loans they have granted to customers, but they also need to understand the varying *risk* associated with these loans—the probability that any loan will turn into a bad debt during a given period. In your human resource (HR) role, you may wish to examine a department's cumulative contribution to the salary bill, as well as its skill mix or experience profile.

Managing Resource Attributes Through Time

If we now raise our perspective to a more strategic level, we need to simplify this detail of the quality profile inside each resource. It is just too complex to try to track every resource item individually—every customer and their purchase rate, every staff member and their experience, and so on—when we are trying to understand how the organization as a whole is progressing.

The Coflow Framework

You may recall from chapter 2 that we suggested you think about resources as being like water in a tank or bathtub, with the inflow being the rate at which water is coming in through the tap and the outflow being the rate at which it is flowing through the drain. The analogy for a resource's attribute, then, is the *heat* that the water holds (Sterman, 2000, chap. 12). The temperature of your bath is simply the total heat divided by the total amount of water.

What can you do if you want more skilled people? Well, what do you do if you want a hotter bath?

1. You can turn on the hot tap to add heat to the bath. The hotter the new water, the less you have to add to raise the average temperature. Similarly, if you hire new people who have much more skill than your existing staff in the tasks you require, then the *total* skill of the group will increase a lot. Since these new people are bringing a disproportionate amount of skill with them, the *average* skill level also rises.
2. The second way to increase the temperature is to use a heater in the bath. (Do not try this at home!) In much the same way, training *directly* adds to a group's skill level. "Experience," by the way, is a special case: Every year that passes adds 1 year of experience to each person in the organization, with no need for anyone to do anything at all!
3. Finally, if there were any way to remove *cold* water, there would be less water left to share the remaining heat, so the temperature would be higher. Resources have a neat characteristic that bath water does not: You can selectively remove only the coldest water (the least skilled staff, the worst customers, the least successful products) and thus leave hotter water behind.

Bear in mind that you will not always want *more* of a particular attribute; sometimes you will want *less*. An obvious example is staff costs, where you may find yourself wanting the same number of people and the same skill levels but face intense pressure to reduce employment costs. It is like having a bath that is too hot and wanting to cool it down. Just work the analogy through again: Let out some of the hot water and run in some cold.

A framework known as "coflow" captures how attributes change over time. The framework gets its name because the attribute "flows with" the resource to which it belongs. Exhibit 4.3 shows a situation where staff skills are being diluted by the hiring of less skilled people. The inflows here are the hiring rate of staff (the resource) and the additional skills they add to the total skill pool. The diagram shows how you calculate, through time, what happens to the *average* skill level. As you add more people with fewer skills, the average drops, following a simple arithmetic path.

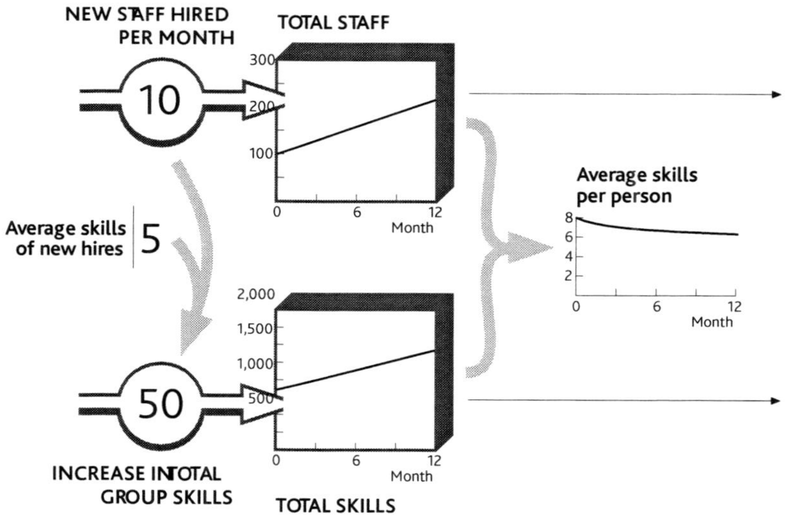

Month-end					
Start	**1**	**2**	**3**	**. . .**	**12**
100	110	120	130	. . .	220
8.0	7.7	7.5	7.3	. . .	6.4
800	850	900	950	. . .	1,400

Exhibit 4.3. Diluting the Average Skill of a Growing Group of Staff

Case Example

The Impact of Offshoring

In the early years of the new millennium, many organizations in western Europe and the United States found they could get critical activities done by organizations with skilled people in India, China, and other low-wage economies at a fraction of the cost of the salaries they were paying in their domestic markets. This opportunity was not confined to routine tasks but applied across a vast range of job types, and enabled many of the companies involved to make important transformations in the way they do business (Balasubramanian & Padhi, 2005). Competitive pressure compelled many organizations to undertake this transition, shedding high-cost people in one area and adding cheaper people elsewhere, whether employing them directly or using independent suppliers. To this rather simple idea, though, you need to add some important complications.

First, the people being lost carried attributes other than salary that may have been important: not only simple skills, but also more subtle knowledge about how your business works. You need a sense of exactly what these other attributes are, how quickly they may be depleted by the transition, and what risks this may impose on the functioning of the rest of the business.

Second, the *providers* in the offshore location understood that offering cheap people was not enough; those people needed to be sufficiently skilled to substitute for those they were replacing. Consequently providers put intense effort into very rapid skill building in the people they hired.

Last, an issue that is not always well understood, there is a limit to just how cool you need your bath to be. China has made a heavy commitment to upgrading its education system with a view to trumping India's ace. China's labor rates in many sectors are still lower than those in India, and its aim for a while was to persuade those very firms who "offshored" to India to move again for still greater savings. But many of those firms had already achieved sufficiently low labor costs that any additional savings was not worth the additional disruption and risk of a second move.

If you brought in people with only three skills each, instead of the five shown in the exhibit, the average would drop faster, to a still lower average level in the long term. You can use a similar method to work out what happens if you lose people with, say, *more* skills than the average for the group. Last, if you undertake training to give each person one new skill per quarter, you would show another inflow directly into the skill resource.

This may appear a mechanistic and artificial way to capture the subtleties of people's individual characteristics, but there *are* cases where skills are clearly laid down and regularly tested. For example, competence tests may be required for people wishing to work as financial advisers or in other professions where the public's safety or well-being are at stake.

Even where you are dealing with more rarefied characteristics in your people, it is important to understand that something very close to this process is taking place. For example, many large companies have competency grids to specify the skills that senior executives require (see Table 4.1). So if you are *not* going to use this approach to work out exactly what you need to do, how much, and when to develop the critical attributes of your people, *how else are you going to do it?*

The last question to consider is, when will the high-level view of a resource attribute (such as Exhibit 4.3) be sufficient, and when do you

Doing It Right

Calculating Average Attributes

You might think that the easiest way to measure these attributes is to put their *average* quantity in the stock that "coflows" with the resource. In Exhibit 4.3, this might mean showing average skills in the resource tank, instead of total skills. Unfortunately, it is just not easy to work out the numbers that way. Think of it this way—the lower tank is keeping a check on the total *heat* in your bathtub; its *temperature* is the total amount of heat divided by the total amount of water.

Tracking the total attribute in this way can produce some curious effects. For example, the attribute stock in Exhibit 4.3 contains the total number of skills held by the group, even though the same skill may be held by many individuals.

need to get into the detail of the quality profile within the resource pool (as shown in Exhibit 4.2)? The answer is to explore the quality of individual resource items in detail if this is essential to answering the specific challenge that you face. For example, is your problem one of inadequate skill across the whole group or a few skilled people and a long "tail" of novices? If it is the latter, then you need to know how many novices there

Table 4.1. Example of a Competency Matrix for Management

	ENTRY	COMPETENT			MASTERY
	1	2	3	4	5
DELIVERY					
Delivering Results					
Perseverance					
Target Orientation					
PEOPLE-RELATED					
Team Working					
People Development					
Organizational Awareness					
Change Management					
INTELLECTUAL					
Analysis and Problem Solving					
Expertise Development					
Knowledge Sharing					
STRATEGIC					
Customer Orientation					
Market Awareness					
Strategic Focus					

are, how much training they need, at what rate they are leaving and being hired, and so on. You may also need to take into account the contributions that the experts can make to improving the novices' skills. In such a case, then, the quality profile curve is an important tool, and you may need to sketch its shape as it is today, together with how you want it to look in 3 months, 6 months, or 1 year from now.

Action Checklist

Using the Resource Attribute Coflow

Exhibit 4.4 provides a "blank" for you to work out how any staff attribute changes through time.

The following steps will enable you to develop such a picture for yourself:

- **Draw a stock and flow diagram for the resource** (such as employees).
- **Draw a second stock diagram below this for the total attribute that the resource possesses.** In Exhibit 4.3, this was total skills, but it could be years of experience, total salary bill, and so on. For a sales team, it could be the total sales rate that the group is achieving.
- **Calculate the average attribute in a chart to the right**. In Exhibit 4.3, it is the total skills held by the employees divided by the number of employees, but it could equally be average salary or average sales per salesperson.
- **Identify the average attribute for resources that are arriving or departing**. In Exhibit 4.3, it is average skills per new hire; in the other cases it would be average salary of each new recruit or average sales rate of each new salesperson.
- **Calculate the increase in total attribute per period arising from this inflow of people** (to the left in Exhibit 4.4). In our examples, this is new hires per month multiplied by the average skill (or average salary, or average sales rate) of each new hire.

- **Calculate the loss of total attribute per period arising from the loss of people** (to the left in Exhibit 4.4).
- **Finally, identify the rate at which other activity** (such as training, salary increases, or changes in sales effectiveness) **adds to the attribute pool.**

These steps should allow you to determine how the group's average attribute has changed up to now, how it will likely change into the future, and what you need to do to make it improve as you want it to.

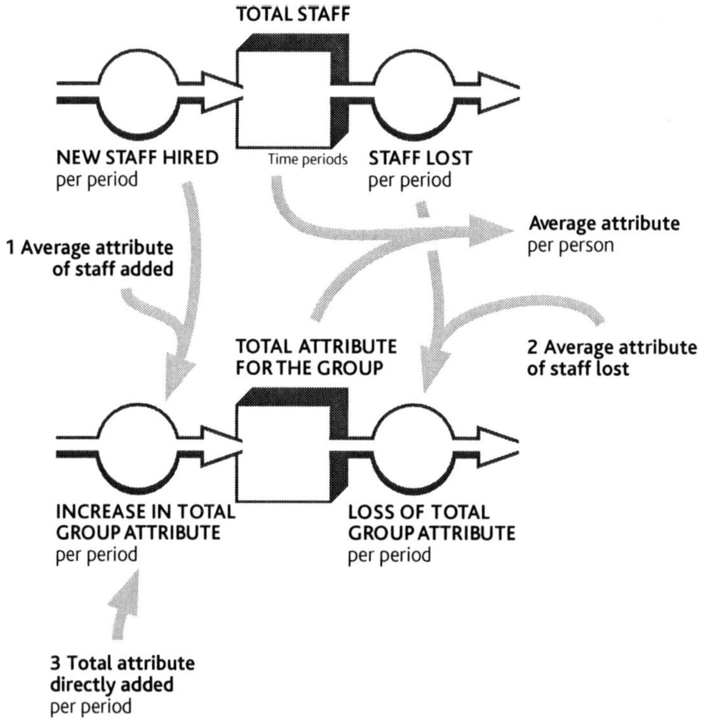

Exhibit 4.4. Generic Structure for Working Out How Attributes Change Through Time

CHAPTER 5

Rivalry for Resources

Overview

We are seldom alone in our desire to capture and develop resources. Competitors will have similar aims, and since potential resources are scarce, we will inevitably come into conflict. Customers are the most obvious example of resources for which we must compete, but staff can also make the choice between working with us or with rivals.

This chapter will do the following:

- **explain how rivalry operates over time**, highlighting three main mechanisms by which rivalry plays out
- **consider the implications of rivalry for human resources** and, in particular, how it affects the ability to attract and retain the best people—the "war for talent"

Three Types of Rivalry

Thankfully, we do not have to compete for all resources. Many physical assets are in plentiful supply from numerous providers who would be only too pleased to supply both us and our competitors. However, conflict *does* arise for any resource that could choose to go either to us or to our rivals (Warren, 2008, chap. 7). Customers are the most obvious example, but staff can be scarce too, especially those with specific skills, and they can certainly choose who to work for. Distributors and other intermediaries are also fought over, as are other types of business partners. Investors and other providers of cash (such as donors for charities) can decide whether to fund us or back competing organizations.

What these resources have in common is that they consist of people with discretion. We are competing for their choices to commit themselves, in part or in whole, to buying from us, working for us, investing in us, or partnering with us. Moreover, since rivalry concerns resources other than customers, it is just as relevant to public sector, voluntary, and other not-for-profit organizations as it is to businesses.

Rivalry for these contested resources takes three distinct forms. To see what these are, take the simple example of Starbucks coffee shops competing for consumers.

- **Type 1 rivalry is the battle to win potential customers**: in this case, people who don't yet frequent coffee shops. Some people have never visited a coffee shop at all, and Starbucks for one would prefer these novices choose one of *their* outlets for their first such experience rather than one of their rivals. If the new customers enjoy their first visit, there is a good chance they will come back again and again. This will be easier to achieve, of course, if Starbucks is the only coffee shop in their area.
- **Type 2 rivalry is the struggle to keep customers from switching to rivals**: a kind of tug-of-war. Having won consumers over to the idea of using coffee shops, Starbucks would prefer to keep them loyal rather than have them switch to using a competitor.
- **Type 3 rivalry is the fight for the greatest share of business from customers who are not exclusively with you or anyone else**. Many consumers will visit other coffee shops as well as Starbucks. Where these customers are concerned, the company will want to capture the largest *share* of their coffee-drinking occasions.

These three competitive processes may operate alone or in combination with each other. Let us look at each in a little more detail.

Type 1 Rivalry: Winning Potential Customers

Exhibit 5.1 shows Type 1 rivalry playing out over time. New potential consumers are constantly entering the picture from the left. Children growing up are one obvious source of this flow, but, especially in an emerging

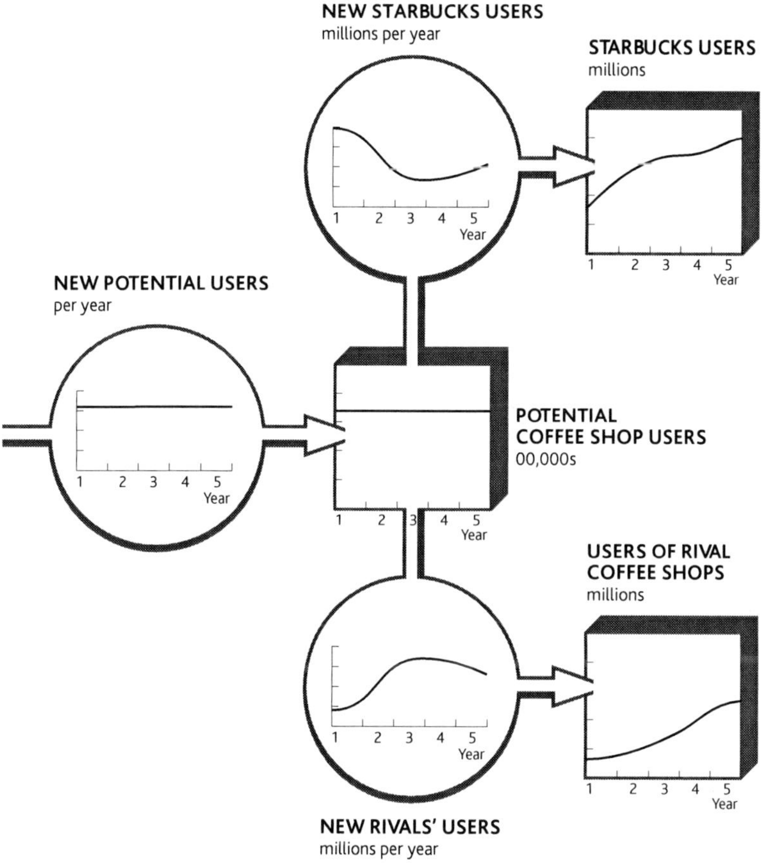

Exhibit 5.1. Type 1 Rivalry for New Coffee Shop Users

market such as coffee shops, adults too will be considering whether they might enjoy a visit to a place they have never tried before.

The first state that people move into is often neglected, but is very important: this is the stock of actively available potential customers. By "actively available," we mean customers who are relatively well informed about what a coffee shop might be like and who feel it could be something they might enjoy. The reason this group is important to identify is that they may be highly receptive to marketing messages encouraging them to take that first step through a coffee shop door.

New consumers in this market are not likely to stay in this "potential" state very long but will soon choose to try a coffee shop, hence the small scale (hundreds of thousands) on the stock of potential users, compared with the millions of active users. The scenario illustrates what will happen if Starbucks initially wins the largest fraction of new users: *Its* flow rate is high and *rivals'* flow rates are low, so Starbucks' stock of users fills faster. Over the next 2 years, the proportion of potential consumers choosing rivals for their first experience grows until it exceeds the proportion choosing Starbucks, so rivals' win rate speeds up and their stock of users starts to fill faster. Note that we have assumed for convenience that there is no outflow of users from any chain (whether through loss of interest, moving away from coffee shop locations, or any other reason).

You will see in Exhibit 5.1 that the stock of potential coffee shop users stays at the same level over the 4 years, even though the total active users for the two stores is increasing. This is because *new* potential users are constantly being created, perhaps because the general popularity of this service is increasing. This will not go on forever, of course; sooner or later the entire local population who might ever like to buy coffee this way will be used up. As the market approaches that point, the inflow of new potential users will slow to a stop and the potential stock will drain away to zero—everyone who *might* use a coffee shop would by then be using Starbucks or its rivals.

Type 1 rivalry is most evident in new markets where customers are being persuaded to commit to a product or service for the first time. But wherever new potential customers are becoming available, they will be fought over in this way, even in mature markets. Any consumer market will exhibit Type 1 rivalry, simply due to the emergence of each new generation of consumers.

Many firms work vigorously to grow the market—cell-phone services provide a good example, as providers put effort into explaining the benefits of each new generation of service. Having persuaded people to become "potential customers," each firm must then fight to win them to their service rather than their rivals.

Type 2 Rivalry: Keeping Customers Loyal

Type 2 rivalry in the coffee shop market happens when regular Starbucks users decide to switch completely to rival outlets, or *vice versa*. Exhibit

5.2 shows what happens if this rivalry plays out over three distinct phases. For convenience, we have assumed that *no* new consumers are emerging during this time. First, Starbucks wins users from rivals, but that rate slows to zero during the first year. Next, the flow starts to increase in the opposite direction, and Starbucks' stock of loyal customers declines as people desert it for competitors. After the middle of year 3, the loss rate slows again until by year 5 there is no net flow in either direction.

There are a few important points to note about Type 2 rivalry:

- **Competition between several rivals can be significant.** Although this is not illustrated in Exhibit 5.2, rivalry will also be occurring among your various competitors. For example, you might discover that one particularly strong firm is taking

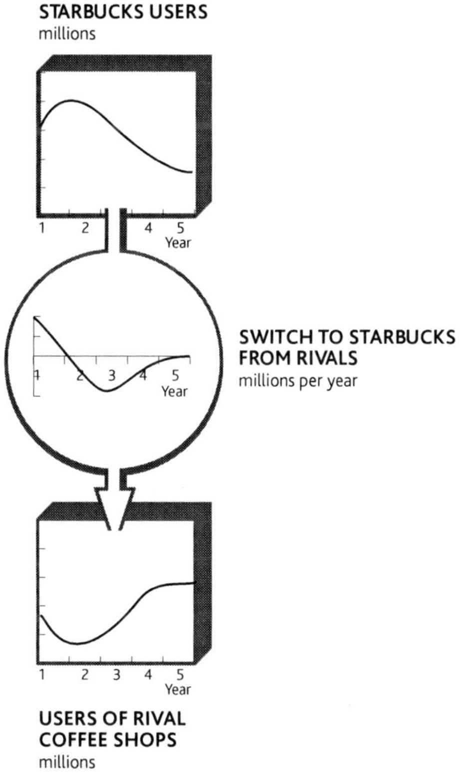

Exhibit 5.2. Type 2 Rivalry for Loyal Customers

customers from other rivals but not from you, so their business is growing while yours is not.

- **Customers may be switching away from you at the same time as others are joining you from rivals.** Exhibit 5.2 only shows the *net* rate of customers switching. However, chapter 2 stressed the importance of knowing the *separate* inflow and outflow rates of resources. Since different populations are involved in these two distinct flows, they may have quite different reasons for choosing to switch. Consequently it is vital to understand both your rate of gains from rivals and your losses to them, as well as what is causing these different flows.

Type 3 Rivalry: Competing for Regular Uncommitted Customers

In Type 3 rivalry, Starbucks battles with rivals for a share of time and spending from those coffee shop users who are not loyal to any one chain. In Exhibit 5.3, Starbucks loses loyal consumers rapidly to this disloyal group. Note that the company's total sales are the sum of purchases by loyal users plus *its share* of purchases by the disloyal group. In this scenario, incidentally, competitors would do well even though they do not grow their loyal user base. This is because the new disloyal group represents a much larger proportion of their sales than it does for Starbucks, a factor that outweighs the limited share of this market that they receive.

Rivalry on All Fronts

All three forms of rivalry can take place simultaneously. In our example, first-time coffee shop users are being chased, efforts are being made to keep customers from switching away (and to encourage the opposite), and chains are trying to grab the largest possible share of disloyals' purchases—all at the same time. Companies use different tactics to drive each favorable flow of customers and choke off the unfavorable flows. Perhaps we might feel some sympathy for marketing professionals who must make difficult choices about how much spending to commit and to which parts of this complex system.

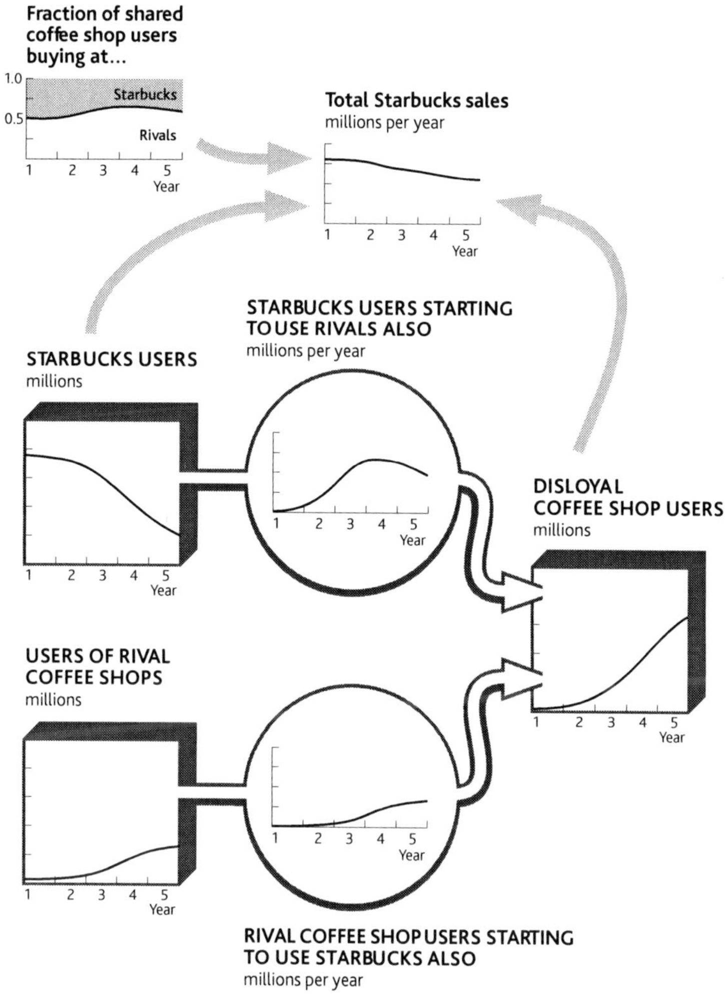

Exhibit 5.3. Type 3 Rivalry for Share of Disloyal Consumers

Chapter 3 looked at how several core resources of a restaurant chain combine to drive profitability. The rivalry for customers in that case operated much as it does in our Starbucks example, but rivalry also occurs for other resources. Good retail locations for restaurants are scarce, and the value of a prime site is immense. Type 1 rivalry therefore operates intensively for this resource. The number of prime sites is limited, and once Starbucks has secured the best sites, only secondary sites are available for its competitors. The other two types of rivalry do not operate for this resource: Once Starbucks has a site, there is nothing rivals can do to switch it to their business, nor can they do anything to share it.

People are the other major resource that Starbucks contests with its competitors. There is a pool of talented potential service staff who might wish to work in coffee shops, and Starbucks would like to win these people before they decide to work for a competitor. In fact, Starbucks' unique staff management and reward systems contribute substantially to their success in this battle. After this Type 1 rivalry has been won, however, Type 2 mechanisms start to take effect. Competitors would like to have Starbucks' best people work for them instead. Few people work for more than one coffee shop, so Type 3 rivalry does not arise.

Competition for people is not limited to service staff. Organizations may face great competition for marketing people, information technology (IT) professionals, and many others. The war for talent can often extend beyond a single industry or sector, as staff may be choosing between many different types of businesses or other organizations.

The extent to which it is necessary to analyze rivalry for employees and review the competitive flows of people depends on how explicitly that rivalry operates. In the case of general service staff, it probably *does not* apply, so it will be sufficient to consider just the flows of staff into and out of your business (as in Exhibit 2.3). However, the more specialized staff become, and the more impact they have on performance, the more the competition for their services intensifies, and the more savage becomes the war for talent. This, of course, is something many professionals seek to promote and exploit in pursuing their careers, as can be seen in many high-profile examples, from football players to TV stars, chief executives to architects. After all, value increases with scarcity, so if your skills are scarce and sought after, then your ability to command a premium salary will be stronger.

Fighting for the People You Need

Organizations facing explicit rivalry for a limited pool of talent will benefit from analyzing in detail how the war for that talent plays out over time (Michaels, Handfield-Jones, & Axelrod, 2001). You have probably worked out already that Type 1 and Type 2 rivalry play a pivotal role in this continuing struggle to win and retain people. But do not imagine that rivalry applies *only* to high-value specialists; it can operate wherever the demand for labor exceeds the available supply.

Consider the challenge you might face if you needed to open a new call center providing sales and customer support. The choice of location may depend on many factors, including the ability to secure people who can fill the various roles required. Few people appreciate just how challenging it is to provide the quantity of trained staff needed to handle incoming inquiries in such centers.

If you had the local job market to yourself, things might be fairly easy. Say you need about 100 staff, and there are 250 people in your area who are either looking for work or not especially committed to their current job. Your recruitment and training team believe they can take on these new hires over about 3 months. Things go reasonably well, but there is one small problem. As you take the best candidates, it proves more difficult to find suitable people from the now diminished pool. Within 6 months you get pretty close to your target of 100 recruits (Exhibit 5.4).

Things work out rather differently if you are not the only organization looking to build a call center in the area. The early challenge now becomes Type 1 rivalry: You will be *competing* to win new staff from that limited pool of potential recruits. With just one competitor hiring in the same market, the pool of good applicants gets used up very quickly, so that by month 3 you have only found about three-quarters of the people you need (Exhibit 5.5, dark gray lines). If you are hiring against *two* other firms, however, things get a lot tougher, and you never get close to your target, given the limited suitability of the last few candidates (Exhibit 5.5, light gray lines).

Of course, you are not alone in suffering this pain. Every competitor has the same problem, so if your rivals adopt an identical hiring plan, their numbers build along the same path as yours.

What might you do about this challenge? Two strategies might work. First, you could make the case for a larger hiring and training team and try to fill the numbers you need before your competitors do. This could work if you throw enough effort at the problem. If your goal is to fill your needs within a month and a half, for example, there are still enough good candidates around when you are filling your last few positions, even with two competing employers.

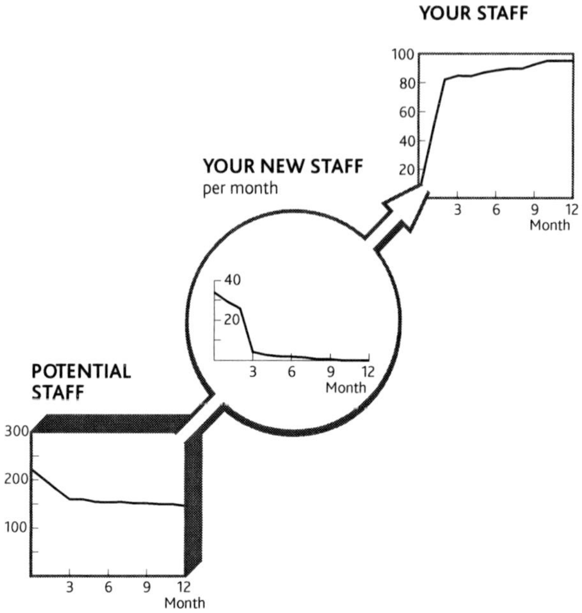

Exhibit 5.4. Hiring Call-Center Staff in a Town With No Rivals

The alternative approach is to poach people from your competitors. With luck, your rivals will not do a good enough job of training and motivating their staff. Some good people could start looking for new jobs, and since they are already trained for call-center work, they are likely to turn to you. This second strategy brings Type 2 rivalry into the war for talent. If you are facing two rival recruiters in this local market, each with a similar hiring plan to yours for first-time call-center staff, you can transform your outcome simply by taking 5% of their staff each month. Just 8 months into your effort you comfortably hit your target of 100 people, while your competitors are languishing at about 60 people each (Exhibit 5.6).

A staff loss of 5% per month may sound like a fast rate, but all it means is that 1 person in 20 decides to switch to you each month, and there may be ways for you to make this happen. Word gets around about good employers; people talk to their families, friends, and neighbors. You can even encourage such conversations by rewarding existing staff

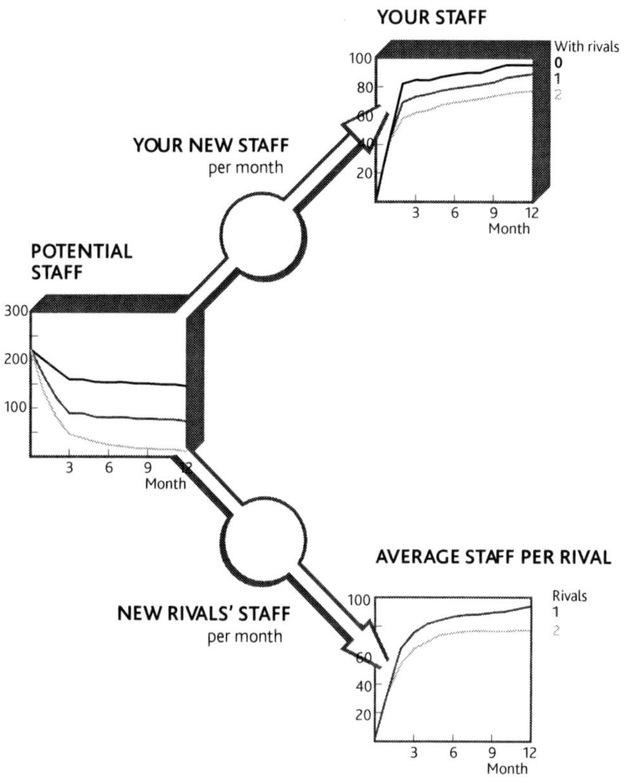

Exhibit 5.5. Hiring Call-Center Staff Against Rivals

for bringing new people over to you. You must be careful, of course, to ensure that incentives are not abused and to guard against your rivals copying your efforts and intensifying the war for talent.

Succeeding in a Competitive Market

Although this example has only touched on the basics of the rivalry for staff, it raises challenging questions that you may need to address whenever you are grappling with a competitive recruitment market.

- Which staff groups and job roles are in limited supply?
- What is the size of the potential talent pool (both people actively seeking new jobs and those who could be enticed)?

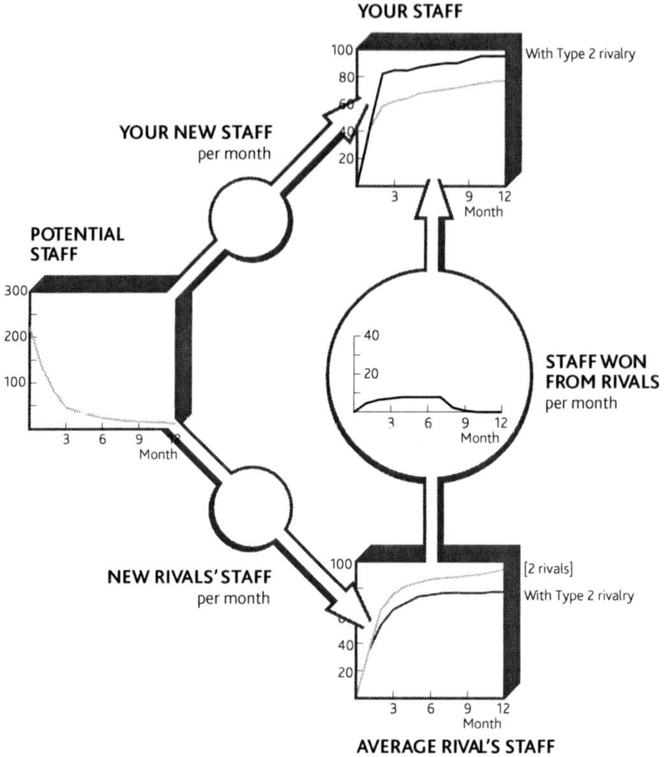

Exhibit 5.6. Adding Type 2 Rivalry to Win Call-Center Staff From Competitors

- Who else is after that talent, how many of them are there, and what is the sum of *their* hiring aspirations?
- How fast could we reasonably expect to fill our staff needs, and what will be happening to the potential pool of staff during this effort?
- What effect does pay and conditions have on our relative success at winning first-time hires and staff who may switch to us? How do we decide on these factors?

In our experience, few organizations have answers to these and other vital questions that affect their ability to build and retain the human resources they need. Few understand just how fierce the war for talent is, even in the most routine job categories. Indeed, so few people today are satisfied with low-level or tedious roles that such jobs can be among the hardest to fill.

For a complete understanding of your staffing dynamics, further mechanisms may need to be added to Exhibit 5.6, such as the following items:

- **The impact of staff turnover.** We discussed the risk of people being enticed away to rival call centers, but there is also the loss of staff from the sector as a whole to consider. In some labor markets, many people no longer see call-center jobs as attractive, and skilled personnel look for alternatives. The need for all competitors to replace these people further intensifies competition for the limited pool of potential recruits.
- **The emergence of new potential recruits.** Fortunately even as turnover removes employees from this role, new potential recruits emerge. This reflects routine demographic and social changes (such as young people entering the labor market) as well as the outflow of staff from other employment sectors.
- **The stimulation of potential new recruits by you and your rivals.** Your hiring efforts go further in their effect than simply winning new hires from the available labor pool. Word gets around that this new job opportunity exists, and this will prompt people to consider moving jobs who had not otherwise thought of doing so. In effect, you will open up a pipe into the left-hand side of the "Potential staff" tank. Your competitors will help do the same. This can work to your advantage: New staff may become aware of the job opportunity through your rivals' efforts, but may find out that you are a better employer. It can, of course, also work to your detriment, with *you* doing the work to build interest in the sector but losing potential recruits to less energetic rivals.
- **Shifting rivalry to trained staff.** Many organizations do not bother hiring novices but instead target people who have already been trained by others. After successfully hiring the 100 people you need for your call center *and* spending weeks training them, you could find that a new call-center operator goes

for precisely these newly skilled staff, saving much of the training effort it would otherwise have had to commit. There will still be some organization-specific training to do, of course, but the basic skill of handling telephone inquiries will already have been developed.

Putting these additional mechanisms together extends the analysis of the war for talent considerably (Exhibit 5.7). If you are to understand the staffing dynamics in a competitive job market, you need some knowledge of all the staff flows in this picture. This sounds demanding, but it is often possible to make reasonable estimates based on what you know about your own staff flows, coupled with well-reasoned assumptions and indicative information on what may be happening to your competitors and the wider job market.

Why would you want to go to all this trouble? To accomplish its goals, your organization depends on having the people it needs in each role and skill area. Chapter 2 highlighted just how serious the consequences of misunderstanding and mismanaging these numbers can be. Because staff development has long-term implications, the damage from staffing errors will not just hit you today but will live with you for many years.

Unforeseen events such as regulatory changes, the advent of new technologies, and the entry of new competitors with different ideas can easily raise the stakes still higher, pushing these rivalry mechanisms into previously unknown territory. You may start seeing staff dynamics that are entirely new, so you need to be able to capture and interpret what is happening—and fast! Only then will you be able to respond appropriately. Indeed, you should consider putting your version of these diagrams on your office wall and track the key numbers constantly.

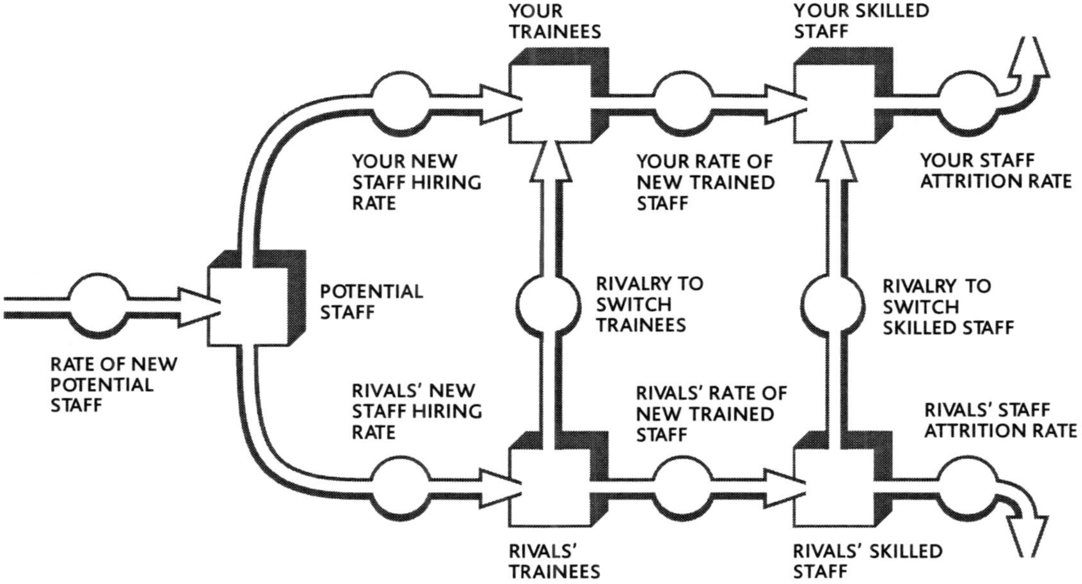

Exhibit 5.7. Adding Staff Turnover, Rivalry for Skilled Staff, and the Emergence of New Recruits to the War for Talen

Action Checklist

Understanding Rivalry for Staff

A disciplined review of the competitive processes surrounding your key staff groups calls for the following steps:

- **Specify exactly what defines each group**. What are their defining characteristics—not just their skills, but also their employment options both within and beyond your own industry?
- **Identify the total reachable population of these people**. How many are there, where are they currently to be found, at what rate are they becoming (or ceasing to be) available, and from what sources?
- **Estimate how these numbers are spread between you, your rivals, and other employment sectors**. Use your own versions of the Type 1 and Type 2 rivalry structures to lay these numbers out, including how they may have changed up to today.
- **Estimate the rates at which people are moving**. Be sure to include the rate at which new talent is emerging, how quickly your firm and key rivals are winning these potential new hires, and the rates at which people are moving to and fro between alternative employers.
- **Identify and evaluate the factors that are causing the people you are seeking to move at these rates.** Which of these factors are under your control and which are not? What effect are they having on switching rates in this labor market, and how might they change over time?
- **Evaluate your options for altering your own activities and policies so as to improve the rate at which people are making employment choices in your favor**. What will be the cost and effectiveness of hiring and developing new talent as compared with fishing in the pool of already skilled people? What mix of these and other alternatives is

best, given their potential implications for future movements among your own staff and those in the outside market?

Repeat these steps for all key categories of staff.

CHAPTER 6

Developing Your Employer Brand

Overview

A powerful weapon for waging the war for talent lies in the reputation you can build up among existing and potential employees for being an employer of choice. Moreover, it is a phenomenon that can and should be deliberately and actively managed at the highest level.

In this chapter we will describe the concept of the employer brand:[1] what it is and how to make it work for your organization.

Developing Employer Brands

The idea of the "employer brand" became fashionable during the severe staff shortages that afflicted technology sectors in the late 1990s, but as that particular challenge faded from memory, interest in the idea waned. This is a shame, since it has a powerful influence on organizations' ability to attract and retain the staff they need (Barrow & Mosley, 2005).

The concept of an employer brand starts with the resource development idea outlined in chapter 2. There we focused on the way people are recruited and then move from level to level within an organization. The status of your employer brand goes further, addressing people's knowledge about your company and their attitudes toward it.

The difficulty here is that the brand values that appeal to your customers may not press any buttons for your employees. On the contrary, they may represent a source of conflict. A simple example is the value consumers place on "convenient" and "responsive" service, which may impose unsocial working hours and disruptive demands on the staff of consumer service organizations. One of the major criticisms of employer brands—and one issue essential for their success—is the need for them to take accurate account of such circumstances. What employees really think about the business needs to be measured and understood and then improved.[2]

The idea of an employer brand is easier to understand if we first imagine a consumer brand company keen to develop loyal customers for a new product—a common process in brand marketing companies such as Coca-Cola or Proctor & Gamble. To succeed in this, the company needs to move consumers through several important states (see Exhibit 6.1):

1. **Unaware consumers must be made aware of the brand** through the use of advertising or other communications that reach out to the pool of people who are not conscious of the brand at all.
2. Once they are aware, **consumers need to understand the brand** and be informed about its benefits and attributes, for example, whether it offers high quality, prestige, value for the money, excitement, and so on.
3. Having understood the brand, **consumers need to be persuaded to buy it and include it in their list of options**. This is where special offers, distributors, and sales agents come in, as well as the people who provide the product or service.
4. **Once consumers buy, their loyalty to the brand needs to be built.** Messages about the brand will need to be constantly reinforced to get consumers to reach this stage and the previous one.

We refer to this process as the "customer choice chain" or choice pipeline (Finskud, 2009).

To build a *new* brand, companies have to move people through these successive states, which takes time and costs money. As always, it is the *flows* between these states that are critical and that we try to "pump" with our advertising, promotion, pricing, and selling efforts. While we are doing this, of course, competitors and other distractions are pushing people in the opposite direction. New people are also entering the chain at the bottom and leaving it from each stage through demographic and other processes.

Just as there is a choice chain for customers, so there is a choice chain to capture people's increasing knowledge of your organization

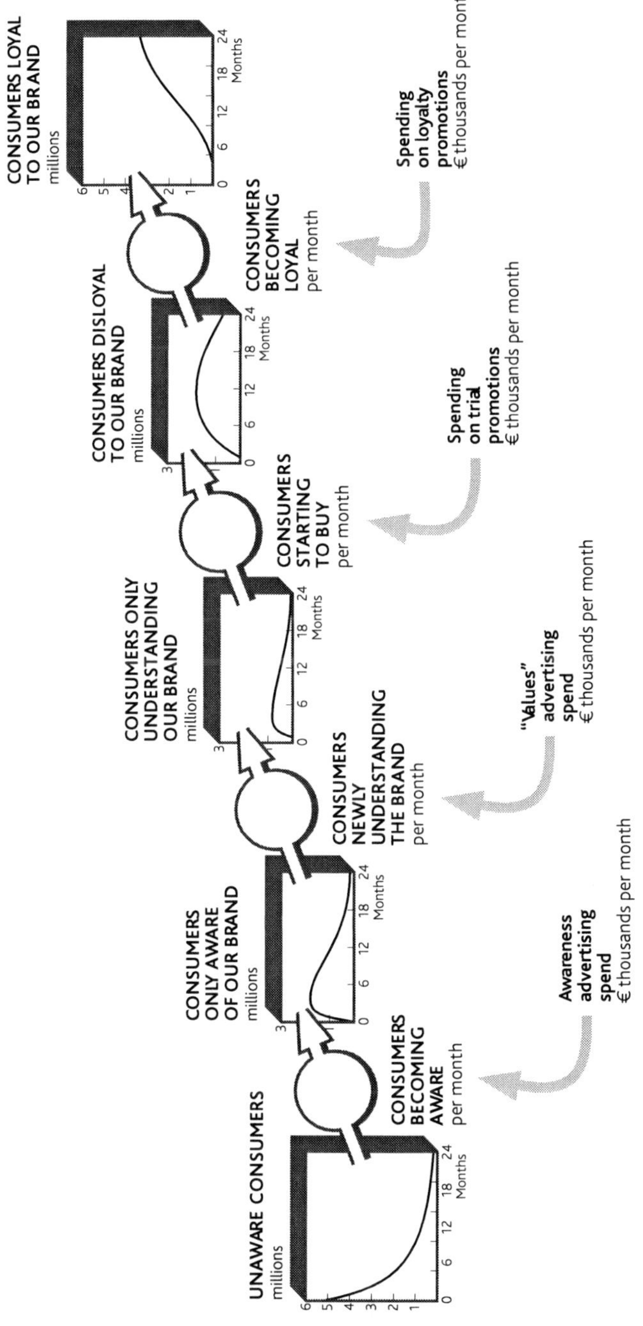

Exhibit 6.1. The Choice Chain for Consumers

and growing commitment to working for it. So how does the process translate from the consumer context to the employee? There are several parallels:

- There is an "addressable market" of people who either work for you or could do so in the role you are considering. For a call center, the addressable market is the total of all employees in the catchment area who could conceivably work for a call center or already do so.
- Some members of this population are unaware of call centers as a potential job opportunity for them.
- Others are aware but do not really know what working for a call center is like.
- A further group understands call-center work to some extent but do not currently work for one. You might want to split this group into a pool of people who have some understanding of the job *in general* and those who have an idea about what working for *you* might be like.
- The last obvious group consists of current employees.

The distinction between disloyal and loyal consumers does not always translate well into the employment world. Most people work exclusively for one organization in a given sector at any point in time. It may, however, be accurate and useful to distinguish between employees who are most committed to your organization and those who are less so and may not be with you for long. Starbucks, from chapter 1, for example, in common with many similar businesses, has a core of long-term employees and a more transient population who come and go. The balance between these two groups can have important consequences for productivity, customer service, and training efforts.

The Employer Brand at Work

The Infosys story (opposite) is a particular example of the challenge facing firms that need to win professionals from a limited pool of qualified individuals. Such situations arise in many different contexts: a law firm

Case Example

Employer Brand Power at Infosys

Infosys Technologies, a world leader in information technology (IT) services based in Bangalore, India, offers an interesting statement on the front of its 2008 annual report (Infosys, 2008): "Our core corporate assets walk out every evening. It is our duty to make sure that these assets return the next morning, mentally and physically enthusiastic and energetic." The first 11 pages of that report go on to talk not about market conditions, customers, or financials, but *exclusively* about its people and what it is doing to develop the potential skill base from which they are drawn.

Infosys has long had a powerful command of the "choice chain" for staff. As the global economic slowdown and dotcom bust of 2001–2002 dragged down most of the IT industry, Infosys defied gravity, increasing revenues by 32% in fiscal year 2002, to US$545 million. Over the same period, net income grew by 25%, to US$164.5 million. While other IT companies were busy cutting their workforces, Infosys hired more than 1,500 people, taking it to more than 10,000 employees worldwide, a number that grew to 91,000 by 2008.

Infosys is able to keep costs down and quality up by leveraging a base of highly trained technicians. Infosys draws in new customers with an array of low-cost software solutions, leveraging its industry-specific expertise in areas such as financial services, manufacturing, distribution, retail, telecommunications, and technology. Its strategy is to extend the life of client relationships in order to improve the efficiency and quality of services delivered and maximize income. Its rock-solid staffing is critical to its ability to continue doing this.

By 2010, a Nasscom study estimated, the Indian IT industry would need 2.3 million software engineers and see a shortfall of more than 20%. But Infosys' efforts continue to boost the availability of talent in the market. During 2007 and 2008, for example, its industry–academia initiative reached 120 colleges and more than 14,000 students. It also trained 871 *teachers*—not only on the supply chain for talent, but also on the supply chain for those who could develop that talent. So challenging is the issue of staff availability that these programs reach out to students in smaller towns and cities to make them employable in the industry.

Developing the available pool, however, would not work if the company did not then capture the people who emerge from it. The company repeatedly ranks as among the most admired companies in India, and talented youngsters regularly choose to work there rather than at global giants like EDS and CSC. The chances of any keen young technology student in India not knowing of Infosys, and not understanding deeply what the company is about, are negligible. Consequently Infosys enjoys a regular flood of applicants, of whom only a small percentage are selected.

needing a specialist in corporate law, a university needing a professor of business administration, or a hospital needing a cardiac surgeon.

In the example that follows, you are entering a new market for professionals in which a few large firms dominate global activity, each employing a few hundred specialists. Your firm already operates in related areas but has no recognition for this particular specialty.

1. **Building brand awareness**. Your first challenge is to make professionals with the necessary skills aware that you intend to build a strong practice in this field. As in our consumer brand example, you can use marketing channels to build this awareness, taking out ads in trade journals, issuing press releases about your new venture, and so on. Exhibit 6.2 shows the resulting shift of people over the early years of your activity. Note that your advertising effort is not the only factor driving an increase in awareness. Professionals will also become aware through their contacts with others in their field.
2. **Promoting understanding of the brand**. Next, the professionals you are after need to understand what it is about *your* activity that makes you an attractive potential employer. You can again use advertising to inform your audience, but you will need to design and script it carefully to convey the key messages that you want people to understand. More intensive communications are also useful here,

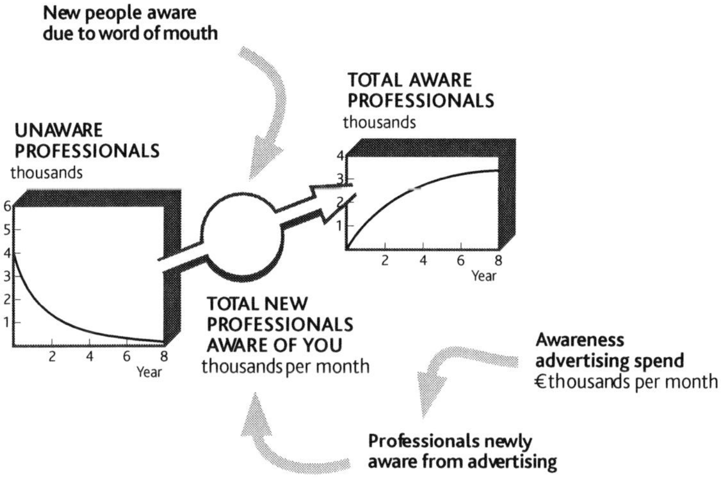

Exhibit 6.2. Building Awareness for a New Employer

such as conference presentations or feature articles. You are looking for opportunities to show what is special about your firm: the particular expertise you are developing, well-regarded individuals who have already joined you, services you are offering, and client segments you are serving.

This activity "pumps" your audience out of a state of mere awareness into a state of being informed. The stock of "aware" people (the dashed line in Exhibit 6.3, which matches the solid line in Exhibit 6.2), is therefore partly drained into the new stock of "informed" professionals. Again, word of mouth within the community will add to this upward flow of people.

3. **Appealing to informed professionals to join you**. Now that you have a population of people who understand what you are about, you are in a much stronger position to appeal to them with job offers, whether through advertising open positions or through headhunting. Without these groups of aware and informed professionals, your hit rate on job ads will be drastically reduced. Why would a good professional keen to develop a strong career in their field want to work for a firm that no one has ever heard of? After a couple of years you have largely overcome this challenge and have a willing audience interested in hearing from you. The rate at which people

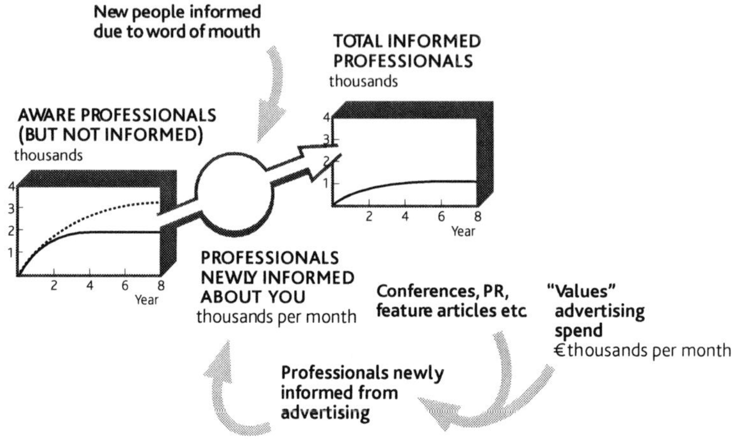

Exhibit 6.3. Building Understanding for a New Employer

actually join you will still reflect the employment conditions you offer and the effort and advertising you commit to your hiring. Existing employees will again help to drive this flow (Exhibit 6.4).

By putting the pieces of this chain together, you get a complete picture of how your staff development effort is progressing (Exhibit 6.5). Exhibit 6.5 helps you with two key questions:

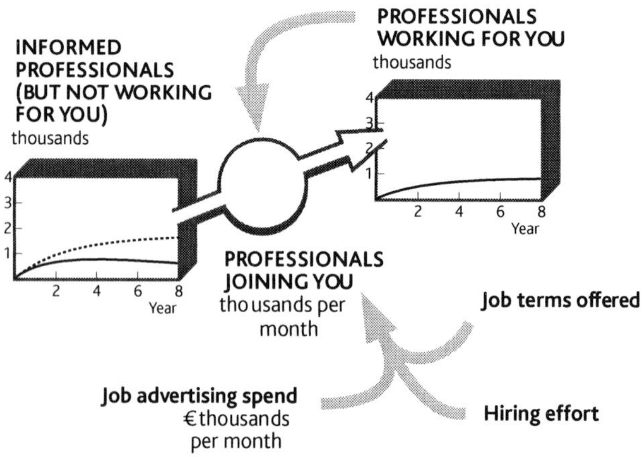

Exhibit 6.4. Winning Staff for a New Employer

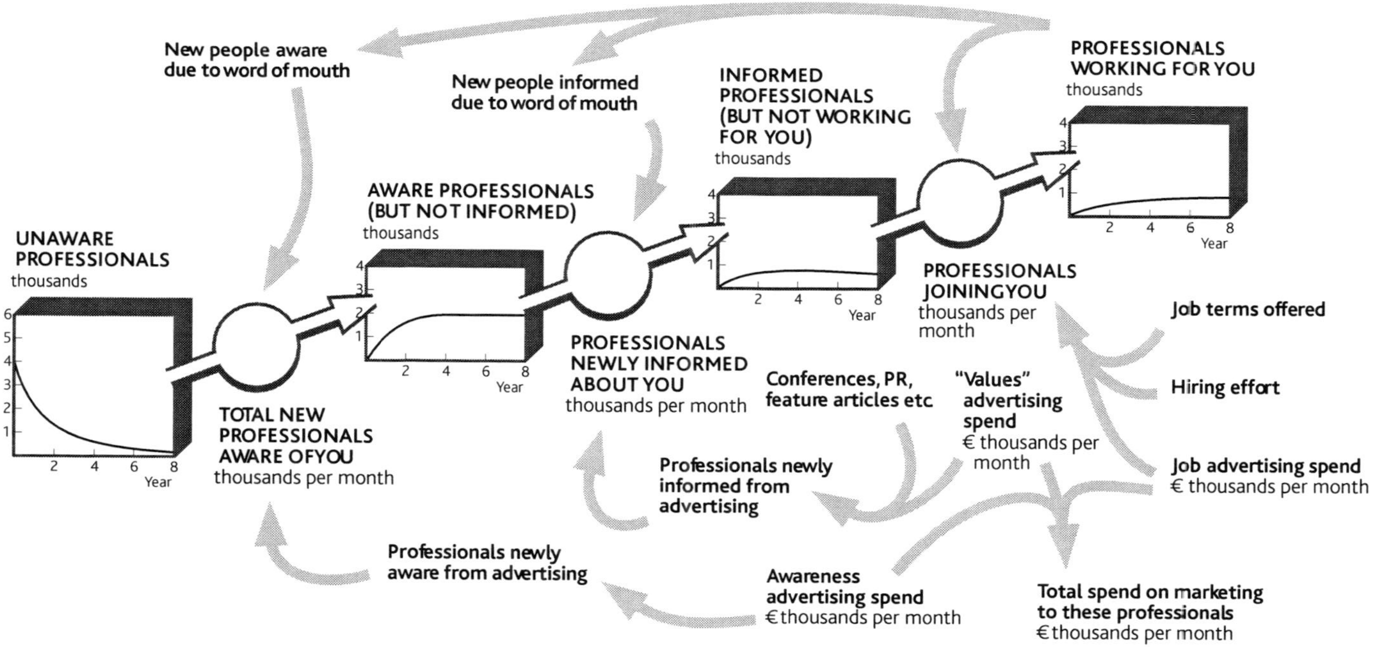

Exhibit 6.5. The Choice Chain for Professionals Joining a New Firm

1. **How much spending should we allocate to each form of communication?** Taking out job advertisements and retaining headhunters are both extremely costly, so it is valuable to know whether this spending is likely to be effective. Spending the right amount at the right time on building awareness and understanding throughout the profession can boost the effectiveness of your future recruitment activities. Note too that you need to estimate how the numbers should change as the new team develops.
2. **How much effort should we commit to which activities?** This concerns not only the human resource (HR) staff but also the professionals you already employ. Building your firm's reputation as an employer through professional conferences, articles, and public relations (PR) makes demands on their time. You are more likely to win their commitment to these efforts if you can show *why* it is important to commit a specific amount of activity and demonstrate the *value* their support has with specific evidence about improvements that are taking place.

Executives often challenge the accuracy with which you can complete the chart shown in Exhibit 6.5, and they are right: It is unlikely that you will know many of the numbers exactly, except for the number of employees and rate of hiring. However, getting the numbers "right" is not the real point.

Take the situation at year 2, where we estimate that 500 to 600 professionals who do not work for you may understand something about your firm's activity in the field (the "Informed professionals" resource in the diagram). Maybe it is 300 or 800 instead, but we are sure it is not 10, and equally we do not believe that most of the 3,000 available professionals are well informed. If you *did* think that only 10 or so professionals understood what you do, then general job advertisements would have a poor hit rate in winning recruits. On the other hand, if you felt that nearly *all* the professionals in the sector have a good understanding of what you do, high spending and strenuous efforts to promote information about your activity would be wasted.

"Values" Matter in Winning Employees as Much as in Winning Consumers

Being informed about a product or potential employer is rather more complex than we have indicated so far. In essence, it means having an understanding of an organization's, or a brand's, "values" (Collins & Porras, 1996; Humble, Jackson, & Thomson, 1994; Kotter, 1995). For product brands, consumers need to understand functional features, such as taste or color, as well as emotional values, such as implied status or sophistication. For an employer brand, both functional dimensions, such as salaries and working conditions, as well as emotional connotations, such as trust and empowerment, are important and must be explained.

This raises the possibility that the values you offer as an employer may *not* fit with those that potential employees would appreciate, in which case you will be doing both parties a favor by making it clear that you would not suit each other. If, however, your values *do* match theirs, the chances of a successful and sustained relationship are substantially increased.

So what creates the employer brand as the person inside the organization experiences it? This is a complex area, but we can identify three important components:

- First, there is **"the deal"**—salary, hours, contract, benefits, and so on—and how attractive it seems to be relative to other opportunities. The deal is the outcome of multiple discrete decisions that are mostly under direct management control.
- The second important influence on how employees feel is the **management or leadership style**. How am I treated? Am I given responsibility? Am I encouraged to develop? Here we should note that although individual managers may be capable of changing their *behaviors*, it usually takes time for their people's *perceptions* to adjust afterward. The gap becomes still wider when efforts are made to change the style and perceptions of that style of a whole organization.
- The third dimension, the factors that constitute what is known as **culture**, is influenced by the other two. How do employees relate to each other? Is there cooperation within and between

> departments? These are matters that shape the experience of working in a particular organization or group and hence determine the performance of these groups, and ultimately of the whole business. As with any other resource, this sense of "how people seem to relate around here" will change for the better or worse through time.

Although perceptions, as we have stressed, are generally slow to change, circumstances can sometimes bring about a dramatic shift in employees' understanding of an organization's values. Such events include bankruptcy, acquisition, and external shocks such as regulatory changes.

It is even possible for a skilled leader to impose deliberate shocks. In one example, an organization that moved to a new divisional structure found that one division head was pursing his unit's results to the detriment of other divisions. Such behavior ran counter to the previous culture but was perceived by some as acceptable under the new order.

One Friday the company's top 200 managers were told to report to the head office on the following Monday for an important announcement. On arriving in the meeting room, the company chairman walked to the front and said, "Thank you for being here. I won't keep you long. Mr. X has just been dismissed as head of his division for pursuing its interests at the expense of the wider organization. This will not happen again. Good day!" No memos, no workshops, no training, no culture-change program—just the pressing of a "reset" button that instantaneously transformed everyone's perception of acceptable behavior.

We will have more to say about intangible factors like trust, reputation, and morale in chapter 7.

Notes

1. The employer brand is a registered trademark of TMP Worldwide Ltd.

2. The authors would like to acknowledge contributions to this chapter from Robert Goodsell of HRG Partners.

Action Checklist

Developing Your Employer Brand

The diagram of how people become aware, informed, and employed by an organization yields a number of insights:

- As with a consumer brand, **people forget or become distracted or misinformed for a host of reasons.** In addition, employees will leave you but remain informed about your activity and what it is like to work for you. In other words, people slip down the chain just as you are trying to push them up it! So as with a consumer brand, you may have to keep up your communications effort even when you are satisfied with the overall state of your staffing and hiring.
- For similar reasons, it is important to **keep existing employees well informed about the reasons people should want to work for you.** It is damaging for them to forget just how good it is to be here, just as it is damaging for Coca-Cola drinkers to forget why they are loyal.
- **Remember the constant "churn" of people through the system.** New young people regularly join the chain at the bottom. The investment to become "top of mind" for emerging young professionals can be substantial, but many powerful firms see the value in reaching and sustaining that status. Again, it is easier to make the case for this commitment if you have some evidence of its value.
- Not all potential employees are the same, **so you may wish to split out different subgroups.** One engineering firm always sought out the best young graduates from the top handful of universities, only to discover that it could not compete on salaries to keep them. Again and again it lost the best people after just 2 years, at huge costs in hiring and training. It learned, however, that it still had large numbers of excellent experienced professionals from universities with lesser reputations. It decided to divert its efforts from a war

for talent that it stood no chance of winning toward attracting a more responsive and reliable employee segment, saving itself considerable cost and effort.

- **Finally, remember that your employer brand may encompass a wide range of potential attitudes.** There are some states we did not show in Exhibit 6.5. Most dangerous are certain negative attitudes that can influence potential staff. Disaffected former employees are the most obvious source, and they can be most damaging.

CHAPTER 7

Intangible Resources

Overview

Intangible resources have a strong influence on performance outcomes, although they do so indirectly through their impact on tangible items such as customers and staff. Knowledge, brand reputation, corporate integrity, and so on are clearly powerful, so senior executives and human resource (HR) professionals must understand how these attitudinal resources work to drive changes in performance through time. In order to *use* this understanding, however, we must go further and understand how these soft factors themselves are built up or lost and what can be done to manage them.

This chapter will do the following:

- **explain how intangible resources achieve the impact that they do**, giving examples of simple measures for them and showing how they operate
- **show how to add intangible resources to your picture of the organization**, deepening your understanding of why it is performing as it is and what you might do about it

The Impact of Intangible Resources

We know that soft factors play a crucial role in competitive performance. Skilled or motivated people perform better, and well-regarded leaders are more able to drive business improvements. It is frustrating, then, that it can be so difficult to demonstrate the value of trying to influence these soft factors. HR professionals in many organizations constantly struggle to defend important investments because there is no immediate payoff in the firm's profits from training, communications efforts, or changes to reward systems. HR is not alone in facing this challenge, of course. Investments in marketing may not be reflected in immediate sales, and investments in research and development (R&D) do not immediately generate new products.

We therefore need tools to demonstrate the value of efforts and investments that are designed to develop strong intangible factors. To accomplish this we work back from our earlier reasoning, that *performance depends on the tangible resources available* (customers, clients, capacity, staff, and so on). Building and sustaining these resources is therefore vital, so if soft factors affect performance—which they clearly do—they *must* do so by affecting your ability to capture and hold on to those tangible factors.

Intangible resources such as morale, trust, and reputation therefore "sit above" this system of concrete factors, influencing how strongly they are won, developed, and sustained. The qualitative impact of these resources seems straightforward enough. For example,

- a skilled sales force will be likely to win new customers faster than an unskilled team;
- call-center staff who feel good about their work should give better service than an unmotivated team, thereby ensuring a higher customer retention rate;
- an information technology (IT) group that is trusted by other departments to deliver good systems on time and on budget will win more requests for new projects than a team that has not earned this trust;
- an organization known for giving staff the freedom to take initiative and for supporting them if they make mistakes will both retain staff more successfully and attract good people faster than an organization without such a reputation.

However, a qualitative understanding is not enough if we are to work out what to do, when, and how much it will cost to bring about some desired improvement over a certain time scale. Hard as it is to detect and manage intangibles, they have another unfortunate feature: They can be *very* tough to manage. You can easily borrow cash, buy production capacity, or hire staff, for example, but it is slow and difficult to build staff morale, a strong reputation, or support from investors.

Measuring Intangible Resources

Before we can understand how intangibles behave, we need some means of specifying and measuring them (Bontis, Dragonetti, Jacobsen, & Roos, 1999; Carmelli, 2004; Lev, 2004; Marr, 2006). Vague comments such as "We have highly motivated staff" or "Our reputation is excellent" do not help us understand performance outcomes in any detail.

Many soft factors seem to exist in a range of conditions from "empty" to "full." There is a good reason why this should be so. Since we are here in the realm of psychological states, we are implicitly peering inside people's heads to examine the activity going on in their brain. "Full" suggests that the maximum mental activity is in progress; "empty" suggests that nothing is going on at all. Most intangible factors can therefore be measured on a scale from 0 to 1. Zero indicates a complete absence of the resource, and 1 is the maximum level you can imagine. This contrasts with commonly used scales ranging from "strongly disagree" to "strongly agree," which mix up positive and negative emotions.

Here are some tips to help you measure intangible resources:

- **Choose the measure that most directly influences the phenomenon you want to explain.** For example, "feeling valued for innovating" will encourage you to come forward with more ideas, so it is more useful in this respect than a measure of feeling valued generally. If staff are leaving because of a known dissatisfaction with relatively poor salaries, then feelings about pay rates are more useful than some general indicator of satisfaction.
- **People are not always truthful.** It is not that they necessarily *wish* to be dishonest, but they may give the answers they think you want to hear, or be keen not to appear foolish, uninformed, ungrateful, or unhappy. They may say they are satisfied with their salary when they do not realize that it is relatively low and then look for a new job as soon as they find out. It may also be worth checking your findings against other information.

For example, research might say that pay is the most important factor for people leaving, whereas you discover that people are actually leaving for *lower* paying jobs that offer other advantages such as flexible working hours.

- **Do not use measures of consequences as substitutes for the true intangible.** This is one of the most common mistakes: for example, using staff turnover rates as a measure for morale. Turnover is the outcome, and morale is *one* of the possible factors driving it.
- **Understand that the baseline for intangible factors changes over time.** Your organization may lead the field in the training it offers today, but if competitors start to provide better training, your previous competitive advantage in the employment market will slip away. Employees may compare their current circumstances with what they previously experienced, with what competitors offer, or with what they think *should* be possible. All of these reference levels may shift through time, so keep an eye on the way they are changing to make sure you are rating your organization accurately.

What Intangibles Do

To understand how exactly intangibles affect the rest of the business system, we need to identify what exactly are the behaviors that they influence. There are two broad kinds of behavioral response that would be helpful:

1. **People choosing to do more of something.** Examples include customers deciding to spend more with you or staff deciding to work more strenuously.
2. **People choosing to switch from one state to another;** for example, new customers deciding to start buying from you, new staff deciding to join you, or investors deciding to fund your business.

Each of these has undesirable counterparts, of course—customers buying less; staff putting in less effort; and customers, staff, or investors deciding to leave.

How Feelings Drive Activity Rates

Let us look first at how intangibles influence people to do more or less of something. Think about a sales force focused on winning orders (rather than an alternative activity, winning new customers). In Exhibit 7.1, motivation among the sales force has been damaged, leading to a decrease in the effort that they put into each sale, and consequently, in the number of orders won. As a result, bonus rates fall, which further hits motivation. The cycle continues until bonuses stop altogether.

While the phenomenon captured here is well known, the diagram brings clarity to what is often a purely conceptual debate. It also highlights common features that are helpful in many situations.

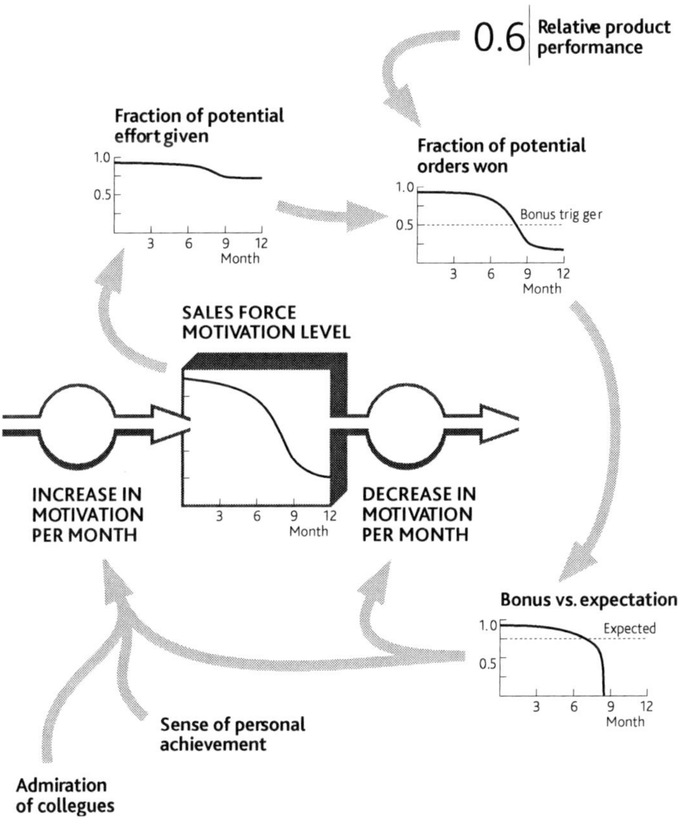

Exhibit 7.1. Motivation Drives Effort and Performance

First, note that just like the tangible resources discussed in earlier chapters, intangibles fill up and drain away over time; this is precisely the feature that makes them resources. So once again we need to understand both how quickly this is happening and what is driving these flows. The resource of reputation, for example, accumulates when satisfied people describe their feelings to others. Staff motivation is increased by events that make people feel good about working harder. In all such cases, the more significant and frequent these events and experiences are, the more the attitude is built up.

The motivation of the sales force in this case is sustained by several features of normal working life—such as the respect of colleagues and a sense of professional pride and achievement—that continually "pump" motivation into the tank. Conversely, other features, such as demands for sales information that are felt to be unreasonable, may deplete the stock of motivation, although we do not show this in the diagram. In this case, one of the causes of the decline in motivation is that the sales team is trying to push a product that does not perform well.

A second common feature of the way soft factors operate is the phenomenon of "thresholds" that can either switch on or reverse other changes. There are two examples in this case, the first being a simple mechanical relationship between sales and bonuses. Bonuses decline with decreased sales performance, but flip to zero below a certain rate of orders captured. The second discontinuity kicks in at the point where bonuses cease to have their intended effect. As long as bonuses exceed expectations, they serve to enhance motivation, but at the point where they slip below the expected rate, they become demotivating. Note that in our example, this occurred *before* bonuses stopped altogether.

Other features may be sufficiently important to warrant the effort to estimate them. For example, the resource of "expected bonus payout" may itself accumulate and deplete. Big bonuses over many months often lead people to believe that these high payouts are normal. Two consequences may result, both of which are unhelpful. The motivation-enhancing effect of the bonus scheme will decline, so that if other factors are damaging motivation, the high bonuses will not be enough to sustain the team's efforts. In addition, a small decrease in bonuses can more quickly switch on a decrease in motivation, so that a bonus rate that would have encouraged more effort some time ago now serves to discourage it.

To get a sense of how much impact motivation and commitment levels can have in practice, it is worth investigating further the Infosys case discussed in chapter 6. Although we focused there on the company's ability to reach out and generate its own supply chain of keen and capable potential recruits, it is clear that its extraordinary commitment to developing and nurturing its people also flows through to very high rates of customer service and productivity.

We have seen another example of the impact intangibles can have on activity rates, this time among customers, in the case of Starbucks in chapter 1. Its most loyal customers use the stores on average nearly 20 times each month—that is, effectively once every working day. The intangible in their heads is a sense of loyalty, specifically a confidence that they will get a great coffee of their preference, served quickly and courteously.

Important though intangibles are to staff performance, it is important not to misattribute success to this factor. Southwest Airlines in the United States achieved outstanding success over two decades, much of which was attributed to a wonderful culture and high motivation levels inspired by the legendary leadership of Herb Kelleher. Indeed, many case studies have been written to make exactly this point. In Europe, on the other hand, Ryanair has been even more successful, and while its chief executive officer (CEO) Michael O'Leary is undoubtedly a powerful and outspoken leader, there is no evidence that the company has built any special culture or motivation levels among staff that show up in any direct link to customer service or sales.

Case Example

Creativity at Google

Like any knowledge-based company, Google relies on the talents and efforts of its staff. In its case, however, productivity is not the only performance dimension that matters. A key principle the company follows is that "work should be challenging, and the challenge should be fun."

Naturally, given its leading position and reputation for being at the forefront of information science, the company attracts a flood of the most talented and creative people and works hard to keep that flood going. However, it has worked equally hard to reinforce and leverage those characteristics among people once they are in the organization. The normal benefits package factors are, of course, attractive, but are no more so than would be expected, so there must be more, and there is. For example, its model includes a 20% time allowance for staff to think innovatively. This is exactly what the kind of people who are attracted to Google enjoy, and it delivers the innovations on which the company is so dependent.

The company is determined to stay a genuinely fun place to work, with such benefits as free massage and recreational facilities including video games and volleyball. Employee ideas are reviewed and implemented quickly, which encourages still further innovation.

How Feelings Drive Switching Decisions

To see how changes in feelings can bring about the second type of behavior, a switch between states, consider a small Web design firm that had been going through a difficult time. Up to this point, strong demand for its services had allowed it to build up a team of enthusiastic and highly capable designers. During a business downturn, activity fell off sharply; clients either closed down or had to cut costs to stay in business. Exhibit 7.2 sums up the history of business activity and staff changes, together with the founder's estimate of how the team's morale changed over the 2 years.

There are four distinct phases to the story:

1. Morale among the team was already falling early in year 1, as the stream of new projects slowed down. Each week that went by without a new project left people feeling that bit more pessimistic.
2. Although the head of the company held on as best he could, he was forced by the last quarter of year 1 to lay off six people. This action hit people hard and some subsequently left. More would have done so if their confidence in finding another job had

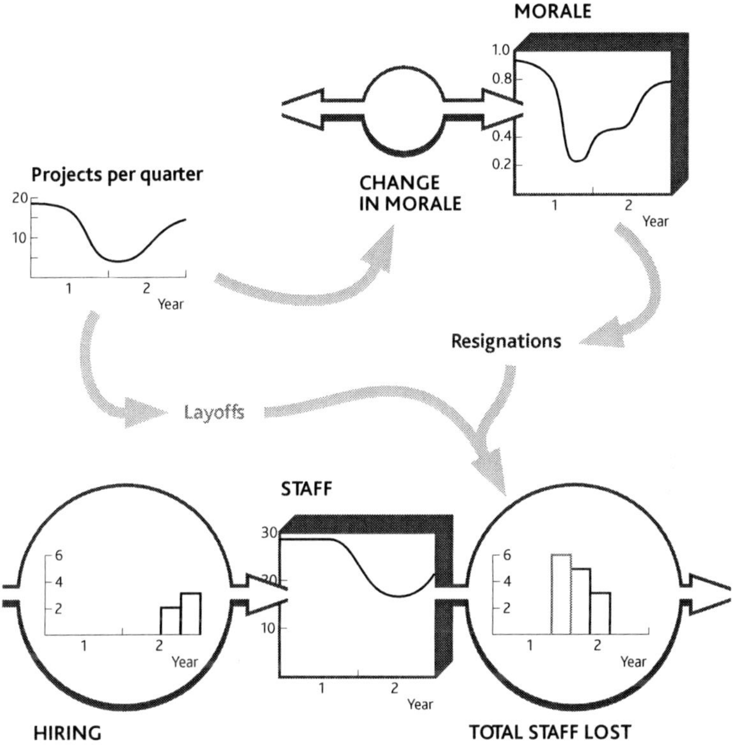

Exhibit 7.2. Morale at a Web Design Firm

not sunk even lower than their morale. (Confidence is another intangible.)

3. Depressed business activity continued early in year 2, and much of the work was rather mundane—not the kind of exciting creative challenge that motivated these people. Morale continued at a low ebb, and more good people resigned.
4. By later in year 2, however, business started to pick up and the firm was able to take on more people.

This story of staff departures exhibits some features that are quite common:

- **Feelings become "filled up" (or depleted) by periodic events.** This mechanism can apply to positive or negative events and feelings: Occasional praise from colleagues fills up your feeling of being valued; unreasonable demands by your boss fill up your feeling of resentment. In Exhibit 7.2, it is *first* the bad news on lost projects and *then* the announcement of layoffs that drain morale. To expand on this idea, Exhibit 7.3 shows the staff dynamics in a team that is subjected to increasingly frequent and increasingly severe negative events.

- **Feelings gradually dissipate.** If praise for your work stops, you eventually lose the glow of feeling valued, and if your boss stops making unreasonable demands, your resentment drains away to a low enough level that an isolated future incident does not make you feel too bad. In Exhibit 7.3, the tolerance limit is reached only gradually because the negative feelings from long ago events have partly faded.
- **The accumulation process separates cause from effect.** Since feelings often build up slowly, there may be little direct evidence that anything is changing. This can create a long delay between the *start* of changes in conditions (here, the date from which the negative events increased) and the resulting outcome.
- **Continuing conditions lead to discontinuities that can seem extremely severe.** The "straw that breaks the camel's back" is a real phenomenon, so be prepared for many individuals to reach the trigger level for action at about the same time.

Given these tricky features of event-driven changes in feelings and behavior, how do you protect yourself against nasty surprises? First, you need to identify the kinds of problematic events that *could* be driving negative feelings. These may include events that are not under your direct management control. In consulting and contracting companies, for example, the loss of key clients or contracts can seriously damage motivation levels.

Next, you need to track what is happening to the negative perception that will eventually trigger action. You need not confine yourself to formal attitude surveys; the best managers intuitively understand how

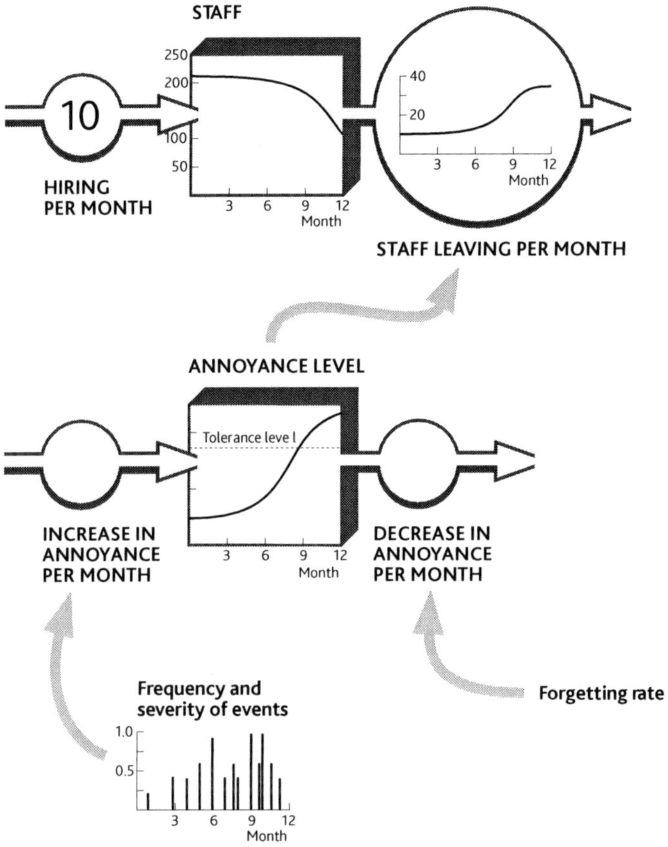

Exhibit 7.3. How Negative Events Trigger Increasingly Rapid Staff Losses

such feelings are changing among their people. Finally, do not forget that resources fill up *and* drain away, so that it may be possible to speed up people's "forgetting rate" of negative feelings. If you have lost a few key customers, for example, reminding your staff that remaining customers are happy and that new ones are being won will drain some of their anxiety. Silence, on the other hand, will leave their stock of anxiety quite full.

Action Checklist

Integrating and Managing Intangible Resources

If you do not know your intangible resources, start finding out! Soft factors *are* influencing your organization, continually and strongly. If you choose to ignore them, you are not actually leaving them out. Instead, you are assuming they are satisfactory and unchanging. This is very unlikely to be correct, so you must make some effort to understand and manage them.

Here are some hints on how to integrate intangibles in your understanding of how your organization is doing and ensure they are working well to support the more tangible elements:

- **Start with a clear and accurate architecture for the tangible core resources of the business.** This may encompass the whole organization and its customers or focus on a single section whose performance concerns you: marketing and sales, or product development. You will struggle to make much sense of the way intangible factors are operating if you do not connect them to the tangibles that they are influencing and that in turn are influencing *them.* Look back to Exhibits 3.4 and 3.5 for examples.
- **Identify which intangibles influence which tangible resource flows.** Since your performance comes from the concrete factors, start with these and ask whether an intangible factor is influencing your ability to win or lose them. Is your reputation as a good employer helping you capture new staff? Is poor morale limiting your success at new product development?
- **Remember that some important factors are negative resources:** things that build up over time that you would rather have *less* of rather than more.
- **Do not try to put everything—tangibles and intangibles —into a single big picture.** The diagrams will be challenging enough for most people without overwhelming them

with all the detail at once! So pull out each key part of the tangible system and place next to it those intangible factors that directly affect that part alone (as we have done with the diagrams in this chapter).

- **Do not search for as many soft factors as possible.** Each resource in your strategic architecture will be influenced most strongly by just one or two key intangibles. You can stop hunting when you have identified enough factors to explain to your colleagues' satisfaction how things are changing through time.
- **Specify each intangible carefully**, identifying the measure that is *really* driving choices by each key group. Getting the right measure matters.
- **Identify those events, actions, or outside influences that cause intangibles to fill up and (separately!) to drain away.** This is exactly the same "bathtub" principle we have used before. Remember that the factors driving inflows may be different from those that drive outflows.
- **Watch out for possible discontinuities** caused by an intangible factor reaching a critical trigger point. If this is a negative phenomenon, look for ways to drain the stock of bad feelings; if positive, make sure to keep the stock of good feelings well filled.
- **Seek the places where actions and decisions can keep each intangible healthy**, or fix it if it is unhealthy. We are not making all this effort just for fun (though it can be more interesting than other approaches to decision making); our aim is to make much better decisions with much greater confidence than before.
- **Estimate the consequences of any changes you make as they emerge through time**, identifying the measures to track to ensure you continue to manage the situation effectively. Choose measures that are most immediately connected to the lever you are pushing. Profit improvements, for example, may not kick in until long after you start a new

incentive scheme, so focus on the immediate productivity improvements first (not forgetting to watch for unintended consequences as well).

- **Build intangible measures into your performance tracking system.** It is best to show these items *connected* to the parts of the strategic architecture that they affect directly. As we suggested earlier, it may be helpful to keep these diagrams on your wall as a continuing tool for planning and assessing strategy.

Finally, remember that staff are not the only group where intangible factors are at work, so pay attention to similar mechanisms affecting customers, investors, and business partners. None of these may be your personal responsibility, of course, but if you can show you understand how the mechanisms work in your HR field, you will be in a strong position to encourage your colleagues in other parts of the business to step up to the same level of skill.

CHAPTER 8
Building Capabilities

Overview

Capabilities are critical to driving and developing resources. They, too, fill up and drain away, and they matter because they determine how effectively your organization is able to build, develop, and retain resources. A more capable organization will be able to build resources *faster, better, and cheaper* than a less capable organization and hold resource losses to a lower rate.

In this final chapter we look at how to build capabilities and explain the following:

- **what capabilities are and how they affect performance**
- **how to develop capabilities** so that you establish a learning organization where people are flexible, adaptable, and successful

Capabilities and Performance

We have used the word "resources" exclusively to mean useful *things* that the organization owns or to which it has access. Capabilities, on the other hand, are *activities* that the organization is good at performing (Schoemaker, 1992; Stalk, Evans, & Shulman, 1992; Ulrich & Smallwood, 2004). Resources and capabilities both display bathtub behavior, filling and draining away over time. We all know capabilities or competences are important, but just as we have done throughout this book, we are going to see why it is important to *quantify* these factors and their effects, and how to do so.

Capabilities determine how well people and groups achieve tasks that are critical to building and retaining resources. Exhibit 8.1 gives examples

Tangible resource	Associated capability	Indicators of strong capability
Staff	Hiring	Success rate, retention rate; suitability of new hirees
	Training	Average skill levels; retraining requirement
Customers	Selling	Customer aquisition rates; quality of the customer base
	Customer service	Fraction of customers lost per month
Products	Product development	Speed of product development; users' ranking of product functionality
Manufactured product quality	Production engineering	Reduction in rate of quality defects
Engineering contracts	Pricing	Rate of contract success; profitability of contracts won

Exhibit 8.1. Resources and Their Associated Capabilities

of capabilities and the resources to which they relate. As for intangible factors, do not forget that it is the *tangible* resources that directly deliver today's performance, so as with intangibles, capabilities *must* operate by affecting your ability to win, develop, and sustain these tangible factors.

We have already seen how hard it can be to measure and track intangible factors, and this problem applies also to capabilities. They are abstract and ambiguous items, posing difficulties of measurement and management. Nevertheless, they are clearly important drivers of performance through time, so some attempt must be made to understand and manage them.

There are three useful reference points to bear in mind when assessing the health of your organization's capabilities:

1. **The maximum rate of resource building or retention**. The best capability in customer relationship management, for example, would result in customer losses of zero. Perfect sales capability would show up as a 100% success rate in new customer acquisition. Perfect employee development might be indicated by a zero loss rate among newly promoted staff. As for intangibles, though, note that these are all *consequences* of strong capability, not measures of the capability itself.

2. **Best practice examples within your organization**. If all your company's product development teams could match division X's time to market, for example, how much faster would they bring out great products? If we could keep staff losses down to the rate that the manager of department Y is achieving, what would that do to our hiring and training load? Note that this benchmark may not rate a "1.0" if we can imagine a still greater level of performances than these teams are achieving.
3. **Best practice among firms in comparable sectors**. If we believed that no retail merchandising team could do a better job than the people at Wal-Mart, for example, we could ask how high a rate of sales per meter of shelf space *they* would achieve if they had *our* store locations.

A good proxy for a team's capability, therefore, is the ratio between the rate at which they are *actually* building the resource and the best rate that we can *imagine*, given one or other of the benchmarks above. So the two key questions become

1. What is the best performance we can conceive of?
2. What can be done to build our capability toward that goal?

Be careful not to expect too much of capabilities. We have repeatedly stressed that resource development depends on the existence of *other* resources needed for that task. Even the most capable team cannot deliver results if the resources they have to work with are inadequate in scale or quality. For example,

- Wal-Mart's merchandising team will not generate high sales per meter if the stores are located so badly that no one visits them;
- the highly capable customer support staff at Infosys, from the example in chapter 6, will not keep important clients happy if the company's systems that serve those clients' needs keep failing;
- pharmaceuticals salespeople will not persuade doctors to prescribe their products if there is no research or articles showing that they are effective and safe.

Since we are viewing a team's capability as an accumulating stock, the questions we applied to resources arise once more: How are they accumulated, and how are they lost?

Developing Organizational Capabilities

There is no great mystery about capability building; it is just a term for what we refer to colloquially as "learning." When you learn something as an individual, you add to the stock of facts that you know or the activities you can do. The only substantial difference for a team is how the *group* accumulates things it knows and activities it understands how to do. The group in which an individual operates has its own stock of facts that it knows (the group's records, routine reports, and databases) and the things that it collectively knows how to do over and above what any individual in it can achieve.

We have established that capabilities are "stocks" that fill up and drain away, so the principles identified for resources apply once more:

- The *level* of any capability can be changed only by some new quantity of capability flowing in or by some existing capability flowing out.
- Inflows and outflows of a given capability depend on the current levels of existing factors, *including the current level of that capability itself.* In everyday terms, the more we understand, the faster we can add to our understanding.

Let us see how this works with an example: the efforts of a small professional firm to build up its stock of clients. Exhibit 8.2 shows the firm's client resources at the top right. Clients are won by the firm's three partners calling potential clients and doing all the things that partners do to persuade such prospects to work with their firm: lunches, presentations, sending brochures, and so on.

At first these inexperienced partners are not too successful; only one-third of their efforts pay off. The time they have to spend on client development is limited, so even if *all* their efforts were successful, they would each expect to win no more than five clients per year.

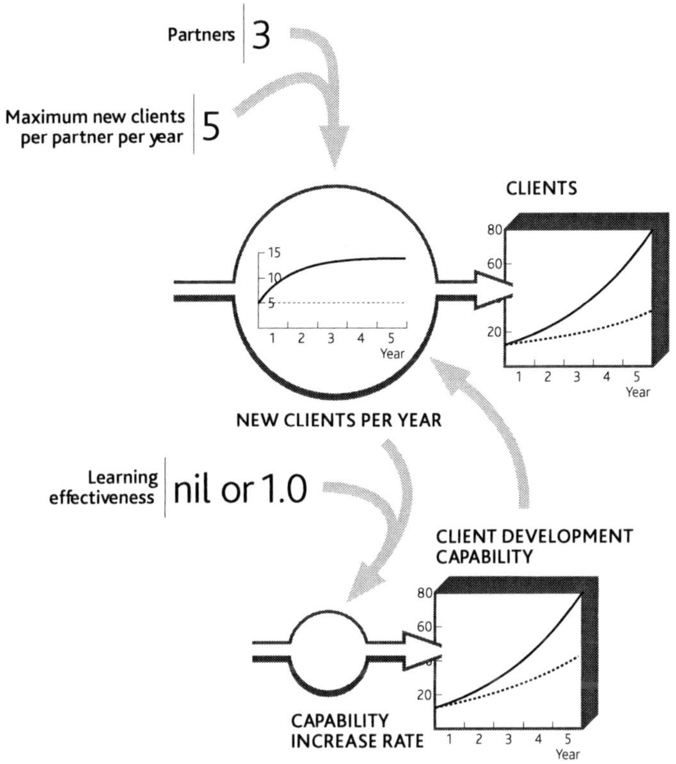

Exhibit 8.2. Building Client Acquisition Capability

In the dotted-line case, they learn nothing whatever from their efforts. Each new client approach occurs as if it were their first. Capability stays low, client acquisition is slow, and the client base builds slowly to nearly 30 over the firm's 5 years.

The solid-line case is quite different. The partners meet regularly and exchange ideas about what did and did not work well with each client contact. They discuss what they have learned about clients' potential needs, how their service can help these clients, and how best to explain the contribution they can make. These discussions "pump" new capability into the group's shared understanding, which then boosts their success at future client acquisition, enabling the client base to grow to twice the level of the zero-learning case.

Case Example

Nokia's Ability to Learn

In the late 1980s, Nokia was a nearly defunct diversified conglomerate known mostly for its rubber and tissue products. Its unlikely decision to put its energy and limited remaining resources behind a minuscule (by industry standards) telecommunications activity, more specifically an emerging mobile telephony sector, triggered an intensive learning culture that still characterizes the company today. In just a few years, this resilient Finnish business learned enough to set the pace in mobile phone design, turning a high-tech device into a lifestyle accessory with a brand that many fashion products might have envied.

The president of Nokia's mobile phones division, Pekka Ala-Pietila, commented, "What we have really learned over the past few years is the very rare capability of putting together end-to-end customer solutions." Speaking about Nokia's strategic thinking process, another senior executive noted, "Of course, we get masses of information, but what is important is that we discuss it a lot among ourselves, kicking it around, looking at it from different perspectives. It is a collective learning process and the key point is whom we should discuss a new piece of information with, to augment it and give it more meaning than it had originally. Then we make some choices, try them out, listen to the feedback, and redirect as needed. With this collective learning process we are all on the same wavelength and we can act very fast when needed."

Nokia has certainly suffered its share of setbacks, but to make a journey from near disaster to world domination in less than 10 years reflects a sustained ability to learn at all levels.

Learning From **Failure** *and Success*

The solid line in Exhibit 8.2 shows our small firm learning from the rate of successful client acquisition alone. It would be a careless group that did not also try to see what it could learn from its *failures.*

To add this to the picture, we would need to add a stock of "active leads" to the left of the clients stock: These would be clients who were in the process of being approached by the partners. The outflow of successes from this resource would pass into the stock of active clients; the outflow of failures would pass back into the outside world. This second flow rate would also influence the learning rate.

Procedures

We saw in chapter 2 that flow rates are critical to building success and thus should be the focus of management attention. The same is true here. Since "learning" is, specifically, the rate of inflow to a capability, this is where we need to focus first. (We will turn later to the outflow, which captures the process of *losing* capability.)

But what exactly is it that our professional service group has learned in Exhibit 8.2? For a start, there is probably some simple factual data such as information about the prospective clients themselves or names of other individuals in these organizations who might be worth approaching. However, this is not what really matters; it forms one of those other resources that may be helpful, but it is not about *how* to win clients. What is going on underneath this learning process is that the group is building up a stock of *procedures*, sometimes called *routines*. For example, "If you ask *this* kind of question, then the clients see that you relate to the problems they face, and that gives you an opening to explain *this* aspect of what we do and how it could help them."

Over their 5 years of collaboration, the three partners have learned many such procedures and discarded others that either did not work or have been improved upon. In all likelihood, they have written down very little of this learning; they are a small group and probably see no need to do so. But what happens if they find they cannot cope with the large business they have built and try to bring in a fourth partner from outside? The newcomer will know nothing of their accumulated experience nor have anything to refer to for guidance. The fourth partner will either have to learn all these things from scratch or be coached by the rest of the team.

Our professional firm's client development process represents a rather subtle example of procedure-building capability. Many simpler and more concrete examples exist, such as the franchise manuals used by McDonald's and other multiple retail groups. If these businesses always left their newly hired people to work out how to do everything for themselves, from fitting out stores to ordering stock and preparing food, they would never have progressed. Instead, they have decades of accumulated procedures written down in the manuals they give to their managers and franchisees. As time passes, new and improved procedures are added and obsolete ones removed.

From a Single Capability to Organizational Learning

It has become accepted wisdom that being quick to learn is vital, not just in one part of the organization, but across all functions and levels, and especially in turbulent times. An organization's ability to learn faster than its competitors is sometimes said to be the ultimate source of competitive advantage. This goes too far—plenty of highly capable organizations have been beaten by rivals with simple advantages they could not defeat—but there is no denying the benefits that can be gained from strong organization-wide learning.

Organizational learning is the total of *all* capability building throughout an organization. It includes not only the processes by which each function develops the resources for which it is responsible but also the mechanisms by which each group supports the aims of others. Firms that are good at organizational learning demonstrate clear evidence of this performance. For example,

- they will exhibit stronger resource flows than comparable organizations;
- they will lose resources more slowly, or not at all;
- they will use widely held and commonly understood processes for getting things done;

- individuals will show rapid learning of functional skills, manifested in their high market value to other employers;
- the organization will be robust even in the face of substantial staff losses. Critical resource flows will be sustained even if experienced staff depart;
- there will be evidence of learning from failures as well as successes.

Proof of the fact that a strong intangible increases the growth of other resources can be seen in the power of *knowledge*. What will matter in the future is an organization's collective skills and knowledge and how they are managed. The success and even the survival of enterprises will come to depend more and more on the performance of their knowledge workers.

Knowledge work is highly specialized. Consider the range and depth of skills and knowledge needed to manage a chain of retail stores, a hospital, a university, a carmaker, or a financial services firm. As the scope and complexity of what we can achieve and what our customers expect deepens, the challenge to keep this expertise coordinated and moving in the right direction grows steeper. The task of employing knowledge in order to meet this challenge is crucial. In the words of Lew Platt, former CEO of Hewlett-Packard (HP), "If HP knew what it knows, we would be three times as profitable."

Avoiding Organizational Forgetting

Amid all the hype about organizational learning, one vital phenomenon often escapes our notice: Like any other accumulating factor, capabilities are vulnerable to *out*flows! This loss of capability, or forgetting, demands separate attention. Several factors cause organizations to lose their capabilities:

- Capabilities simply decay as individuals ignore or simply forget procedures.
- Procedures become obsolete.
- Employees who leave a firm take with them some of the organization's knowledge (although a strong team capability should be somewhat resilient to such losses).

Case Example

Skandia: Knowledge Matters

One of the first people to quantify and value intellectual capital was Leif Edvinsson, appointed in 1991 as the world's first director of intellectual capital at Skandia, Sweden's largest financial services corporation. Edvinsson's approach classifies intellectual capital in three categories:

1. **Human capital**, what is in the heads of employees
2. **Structural capital**, what remains in the organization
3. **Customer capital**, what derives from the relationships that the company enjoys with its customers. Customer capital is often seen as a subset of structural capital.

Skandia uses measures to track whether intellectual capital is increasing or decreasing and focuses its culture and thinking on boosting its intangible assets. In Edvinsson's view, "Intellectual capital is a combination of human capital—the brains, skills, insights, and potential of those in an organization, and structural capital—things like the processes wrapped up in customers, processes, databases, brands, and systems. It is the ability to transform knowledge and intangible assets into wealth-creating resources by multiplying human capital with structural capital. This is the intellectual capital multiplier effect."

At Skandia, human capital is divided further into customer focus, process focus, and renewal and development focus. Each business unit uses a process designed by Edvinsson to report on all of these areas of intellectual capital. The effect of his work has been remarkable: In its annual report, the company puts the value of its intangible intellectual capital assets at more than $15 billion. However, for Edvinsson the real benefit was even greater: Managing intellectual capital nurtured innovation and fresh thinking and helped create a mindset that would enable Skandia to compete in the future.

These losses are endemic and largely unavoidable. However, a strong organization makes sure that its processes and procedures—"the way we do things around here"—are constantly replenished and repaired. Unfortunately organizations can perversely inflict major losses of capability on themselves in a number of ways.

The first is by **cost cutting**. An obsession with cost reduction can easily do away with people, infrastructure, and procedures that together make up critical capabilities. Such losses increase pressures on remaining staff, who then perform at less than their best or leave altogether. Before long, the tendency to lose capabilities can become institutionalized, even when staff manage to find the time and space to create new capabilities in the first place.

A related threat to capabilities arises from **short-term views of shareholder value**. An undue focus on quarterly earnings inevitably drives managers to bear down on those people, activities, and costs that do not quickly deliver profitability. This has at least three detrimental effects:

1. It eliminates the organizational space in which capability can be built so as to drive future performance. People have neither the time nor the motivation to do anything but act for immediate or short-term benefit.
2. It may push management into destroying the firm's existing capabilities, invariably with the cry, "That's just overhead; we can cut that group out." It is worth considering how few firms have actually managed to cut their way to profit growth.
3. Short termism blinds managers to the virtuous cycle leading from capability building to resource development and from there to future earnings. No one sticks around long enough to see things through.

The third way capabilities are eroded and lost arises from another fashionable obsession, for **reorganization and transformation**. Overly rapid movement of people and groups and constant redefinition of what you want them to do all result in the loss of critical capabilities. Having devoted individual and collective effort to developing great ways to get things done, the organization moves people on and the incomers set about reinventing solutions to precisely the same challenges all over again (if, of course, they even appreciate that the need exists). Such cavalier management does further damage to critical intangibles: It is extremely demoralizing to work hard at important tasks only to be moved on and discover later that your efforts have been ignored, with your replacement starting from scratch to achieve what you had figured out long ago.

Case Example

From R&D to "C&D" at Proctor & Gamble

Few companies can match the outstanding product development capability of consumer goods company Proctor & Gamble (P&G; Huston & Sakkab, 2006). For decades, this worked just fine on the basis of internal research and development (R&D), but by 2000 it became clear that this invent-it-ourselves model would not continue to deliver the required returns. The success rate of new product launches was stuck at 35%, sales growth stopped, and earnings fell.

Key to tackling this challenge was recognizing that innovation did not have to rely only on *internal* capability. The company already knew that its greatest successes had come from connections between internal business units and departments and asked itself whether the same principle could be extended outside the organization. For every R&D professional within the company, there were hundreds of people—scientists and engineers especially—working on the same issues in other organizations. Furthermore, the highest innovation rates were coming from smaller firms. P&G set up Connect and Develop, or C&D, deliberately to source innovations from outside the corporation, aiming for half of its innovations to come *through* its labs, on top of the half that came *from* them.

Action Checklist

Keeping Capabilities Strong

When a resource fails to develop satisfactorily, there may be a host of possible reasons. This makes it vital to have a process for diagnosing the source of problems and identifying solutions. The first steps are to

- identify the problem or opportunity;
- trace the problem back to a resource that is not developing as it should over time;
- find out whether this failure to develop flows from inadequate acquisition or excessive losses.

You should then apply the following process to any such problematic resource flow:

- **Check whether the resource-building challenge really results from weak capabilities.** For example, if you are failing to win the specialist staff you need, your lack of reputation among potential applicants could be the reason rather than deficiencies in your recruitment procedures. If customer losses are occurring too quickly, aggressive rivals offering irresistible terms could be to blame and not poor customer support capabilities.
- **To maintain a strong capability, specify what "strong" looks like.** Once you believe that an important capability might not be strong enough, work to understand what constitutes a strong capability. What tasks and processes have to be undertaken? Which of them is not functioning as well as it could or should?
- **Formalize strong procedures—as far as it is worthwhile.** Document powerful procedures and use them as the basis for training and performance control. You cannot formalize everything though. Many group processes are fluid and rely on interpersonal understanding that is too subtle to specify.

Others make a trivial contribution to performance or arise so rarely that it is not worth the time and effort to document them.

- **Maintain a library of procedures.** There is a strong tendency to add new methods when new needs arise. If this practice continues, the result is a massive pile of information about how to do things, most of which is obsolete. So make sure the manuals or systems you use to capture a group's capabilities are regularly thinned out.
- **Make sure you are trying to build the right capabilities.** If you devote huge efforts to building great product development capability, say, it will be disappointing to find that every innovation you bring out is beaten by rivals who did not bother with product development but simply licensed products from others. Personal computer (PC) producer Dell illustrates the opposite case: deciding what *not* to try for. Since it focuses almost exclusively on selling its products direct to users, it has no need to assemble retailer management capabilities.

Going Forward

This book has introduced the essential elements of strategy dynamics as they apply to people-related issues in businesses and other organizations. In an effort to make the ideas accessible to the widest possible range of people, we have kept the book short and the examples easy to follow. We have also simplified or left out many features and details of the approach, while retaining the most powerful elements.

As with any methodical approach to management issues, it is much easier to make progress if everyone involved shares the same understanding, so it is helpful to develop a coalition of colleagues who have picked up the ideas and tried using them. Equally, it can be difficult to win support for new efforts when there is so much else going on around you. It is best to start small, perhaps using just one or two of the most useful frameworks from this book to work on specific challenges. As confidence grows, you can seek support for doing more.

There is much more to be learned about how an organization's performance develops through time and how professional strategic management can drive big improvements to this trajectory.

Another short book, Kim Warren's *Building Strategy and Performance Through Time* (2009), provides guidance on how general managers and their teams can understand their organization's performance and drive it into the future. Those wishing to study the underlying method in more depth should see his book *Strategic Management Dynamics* (2008).

The implications for marketing and brand strategy are well understood and have been put to good use in many businesses (see *Developing Winning Brand Strategies* [Finskud, 2009]). Learning materials, including a 10-class online course, simulation-based exercises, and worksheets are available from Strategy Dynamics Ltd. at http://www.strategydynamics.com. These are designed for individual and team study, as well as for business school degree courses and executive training.

References

Balasubramanian, R., & Padhi, A. (2005). The next wave in U.S. offshoring. *McKinsey Quarterly, 1*, 6–9.

Barrow, S., & Mosley, R. (2005). *The employer brand: Bringing the best of brand management to people at work*. Chichester, UK: John Wiley & Sons.

Bontis, N., Dragonetti, N., Jacobsen, K., & Roos, G. (1999). The knowledge toolbox: A review of the tools available to measure and manage intangible resources. *European Management Journal, 17(4)*, 391–402.

Carmelli, A. (2004). Assessing core intangible resources. *European Management Journal, 22*(1), 110–122.

Collins, J., & Porras, J. (1996). Building your company's vision. *Harvard Business Review, 74*(5), 65–77.

Collis, D. J., & Montgomery, C. A. (1994). Competing on resources: Strategy in the 1990s. *Harvard Business Review, 74*(4), 118–128.

de Geus, A. (1988). Planning as learning. *Harvard Business Review, 66*(2), 70–74.

Doman, A., Glucksman, M., Tu, N., & Warren, K. (2000). The talent growth dynamic. *McKinsey Quarterly, 1*, 106–115.

Edvinsson, L., & Malone, M. (1997). *Intellectual capital: Realizing your company's true value by finding its hidden brainpower*. New York: Harper Business.

Finskud, L. (2009). *Competing for choice*. Williston, VT: Business Expert Press.

Forrester, J. W. (1961). *Industrial dynamics*. Cambridge, MA: Productivity Press.

Humble, J., Jackson, D., & Thomson, A. (1994). The strategic power of corporate values. *Long Range Planning, 27*(6), 28–42.

Huston, L., & Sakkab, N. (2006). P&G's new innovation model. *Harvard Business School, Working Knowledge*. Retrieved November 20, 2008, from http://hbswk.hbs.edu/archive/5258.html

Infosys. (2008). *Annual Report 2008*. Retrieved December 5, 2008, from http://www.infosys.com/investors/reports-filings/annual-report/

Kaplan, R. S., & Norton, D. P. (2004). *Strategy maps: Converting intangible assets into tangible outcomes*. Boston: Harvard Business Press.

Kotter, J. (1995). Leading change: Why transformation efforts fail. *Harvard Business Review, 73*(2), 59–67.

Lev, B. (2004). Sharpening the intangibles edge. *Harvard Business Review, 82*(6), 109–118.

Maister, D. (2003). *Managing the professional service firm.* London: Simon & Schuster.

Marr, B. (2006). *Strategic performance management: Leveraging and measuring your intangible value drivers.* Burlington, MA: Elsevier.

Michaels, E., Handfield-Jones, H., & Axelrod, B. (2001). *The war for talent.* Boston: Harvard Business School Publishing.

Schoemaker, P. J. H. (1992). How to link strategic vision to core capabilities. *Sloan Management Review, 34*(1), 67–81.

Schuler, R. S., & Jackson, S. E. (Eds.). (2007). *Strategic human resource management.* Oxford: Blackwell.

ShiftyStuporvisor. (2007, March 3). Starbucks chairman warns of "the commoditization of the Starbucks experience" [Comment 30]. *Starbucks Gossip.* Message posted to http://starbucksgossip.typepad.com/_/2007/02/starbucks_chair_2/comments/page/3/

Stalk, G., Evans, P., & Shulman, L. (1992). Competing on capabilities. *Harvard Business Review,* 70(2), 57–69.

Sterman, J. D. (2000). *Business dynamics.* New York: McGraw-Hill.

Ulrich, D., & Smallwood, N. (2004). Capitalizing on capabilities. *Harvard Business Review, 82*(6), 119–127.

van der Heijden, K. (2005). *Scenarios: The art of strategic conversation* (2nd ed.). Chichester, UK: John Wiley & Sons.

Warren, K. D. (2008). *Strategic management dynamics.* Chichester, UK: John Wiley & Sons.

Warren, K. D. (2009). *Building strategy and performance through time.* Williston, VT: Business Expert Press.

Weber, G. (2005, February). Preserving the Starbucks counter culture. *Workforce Management,* 28–34. Retrieved November 12, 2008, from http://www.workforce.com/section/06/feature/23/94/44/

Index

Note: The italicized *e* or *t* following page numbers refers to exhibits or tables, respectively.